Samsung Galaxy Tab S9 Series User Guide

The Most Complete Step by Step Manual to Mastering the Latest Samsung Galaxy Tab S9, S9 Ultra and S9 Plus Hidden Features and Updates with Useful Tips & Tricks

D1522580

Perry

Hoover

Disclaimer

The information in this book is based on personal experience and anecdotal evidence. Although the author has made every attempt to achieve an accuracy of the information gathered in this book, they make no representation or warranties concerning the accuracy or completeness of the contents of this book. Your circumstances may not be suited to some illustrations in this book.

The author disclaims any liability arising directly or indirectly from the use of this book. Readers are encouraged to seek Medical. Accounting, legal, or professional help when required.

This guide is for informational purposes only, and the author does not accept any responsibilities for any liabilities resulting from the use of this information. While every attempt has been made to verify the information provided here, the author cannot assume any responsibility for errors, inaccuracies or omission.

Printed in the United States of America

Table of Contents

INTRODUCTION

The most recent Galaxy Tabs released by Samsung are without a question the best Android tablet now available for purchase. They are superior in terms of raw performance, display quality, and battery life, leaving behind very little competition.

Tab S9, Tab S9+, and Tab S9 Ultra are the three different tablets that are included in the Tab S9 series. There are some subtle differences between them, despite the fact that they have many of the same internal components, including the Qualcomm Snapdragon 8 Gen 2 CPU. For instance, the Tab S9 has 8 gigabytes of RAM, whereas the Tab S9+ and the Tab S9 Ultra each have 12 gigabytes of RAM. In addition, the S9 Ultra comes with a secondary front camera that improves the quality of video calls. The screen size is the key aspect that differentiates these three tablets: the Tab S9 has an

11-inch screen, the Tab S9+ has a 12.4-inch screen, and the Tab S9 Ultra has a 14.6-inch screen. Your plans for using the gadget should play a significant role in your decision.

Let's get one thing straight before we go any farther with this discussion. These tablets are more than capable of dealing with responsibilities associated with work. (In point of fact, I am producing this evaluation on the Samsung Galaxy Tab S9 Ultra.) Recent updates to Android's capabilities for tablets have made multitasking easier by introducing a mode called split-screen, and Samsung now allows users to run a third app in a window that floats between the two primary windows. This app may be quickly accessed by sliding it to the edge of the screen or minimizing it into a floating bubble. This feature is perfect for apps that allow users to send messages or stream music. It's even feasible to run two different tabs in Chrome at the same time side by side.

In addition to that, I am presently making use of Samsung's DeX mode in conjunction with a Bluetooth keyboard. This mode, which is accessible on Galaxy mobile devices, has an interface that is more comparable to that of a desktop computer. It includes a taskbar at the bottom and resizable program windows, similar to what one would see in the Windows or macOS operating systems. You can also connect the Tab S9 series wirelessly to Windows computers to use as a second screen, or you can use the tablet in conjunction with an external monitor to create a dual-screen arrangement.

When it comes to the hardware, the AMOLED displays found on the Tab S9 series have a refresh rate of 120 Hz, making them very brilliant, bright, and clear. The audio quality produced by the quad speakers is remarkable, although some songs sounded less full when compared to how they were rendered on the iPad Pro.

Each Tab S9 comes with a S Pen stylus that is rated IP68, a first for the company's tablet lineup, and a microSD card slot for expanding the storage capacity of the device. When using note-taking applications like Goodnotes and Samsung Notes, which are both free for the first year, I discovered that the stylus was helpful. Additionally, it worked quite well for drawing, despite the fact that I don't sketch nearly as much as I used to.

The option to store and charge the S Pen by placing it on the back of the tablet in either the vertical or horizontal orientation is a significant improvement.

Without further ado, I would suggest going with either the Tab S9+ or the Tab S9 Ultra if you intend to utilize the Tab S9 series for both professional and personal purposes. There aren't very many Android tablets with large screens on the market, so the

Ultra, which is quite a little bigger than other tablets, sticks out as being particularly unusual. It really is a matter of "going big or going home," isn't it?

CHAPTER ONE

New Features of Samsung Tab S9

After a little lull, Samsung has finally introduced the much anticipated successor to the Galaxy Tab S8 tablet, which was initially released in 2021. This new tablet is smaller than its predecessor but still packs a powerful punch.

So, what has Samsung been able to do during this time of transition? The Galaxy Tab S9 is, in essence, a big evolutionary leap. It addresses many of the flaws of Samsung's earlier compact tablets and propels the compact Android slate to new heights. This is due to the fact that it features a larger display than its predecessors. A truly sumptuous user experience has been created as a consequence of significant improvements made to fundamental areas of the tablet experience. These fundamental aspects include the display, performance, and audio quality of the tablet.

The all-new Galaxy Tab S9 is an absolute joy to use. It has all the features and complexity that you would anticipate from a Samsung device with a larger screen, but it manages to keep a size that is aesthetically compact in comparison to the other tablets in the new Galaxy Tab S9 series. This makes the all-new Galaxy Tab S9 an excellent choice for anybody looking for a tablet.

The question now is, what precisely has changed, and should you seriously consider upgrading from an older Samsung tablet you already own?

What's new about this device?

Organic light Emitting dio

- Introducing the new 11" AMOLED display, replacing the previous LCD screen.

Liq Crystal?

2

- Equipped with the latest Snapdragon 8 Gen 2 Galaxy chipset.
- Boasting <u>IP68</u> water resistance for added ? durability.
- Enhanced speakers for a more immersive audio experience.
- Featuring a single rear camera with a sleek design reminiscent of the Galaxy S23.

Unboxing

What comes in the Galaxy Tab S9 package? Inside, you'll discover:

- Samsung Galaxy Tab S9 tablet
- S Pen stylus

- USB-C charging cable
- Leaflets and user manuals *Never seen*

Specs

As was noted earlier, the Galaxy Tab S9 comes equipped with a number of noteworthy improvements to its hardware. The most notable of these is the debut of a brand-new AMOLED display, which is the first time that this particular technology has been implemented in a portable Samsung tablet. LCD displays were utilized in every basic Galaxy Tab until this point. Additionally, the presence of the flagship-grade Snapdragon 8 Gen 2 chip provides top-notch performance, which enables the Galaxy Tab S9 to deliver remarkable performance that is beyond its size and weight class. This is made possible by the tablet's ability to:

Dimensions:

- 165.8 x 254.3 x 5.9mm

7.4   10

Weight:

- (Wi-Fi): 498g, (5G): 500g

Operating System (OS):

- Android 13 for all models

Display:

- 11-inch Dynamic AMOLED 2X

Refresh Rate:

- All Models: 120Hz

CPU:

- All Models: Snapdragon 8 Gen 2 for Galaxy

RAM:

- 8GB, 12GB options

Storage:

- 128GB, 256GB options

Battery:

- 8,400mAh

Rear Cameras:

- 13MP main

Front Cameras:

- 12MP ultra-wide

Design and Colors

The design of the Galaxy Tab S9 is consistent with that of its forerunners, the Galaxy Tab S8 and the Galaxy Tab S7, and so is instantly recognizable. It has a refined appearance that cannot be denied, and its slim, rectangular shape makes it unquestionably appealing.

It is easy to comprehend why Samsung would choose to maintain this tried and tested layout. As a consequence, it produces a device that is not only lightweight but also very compact, making it an extremely appealing product. The bezels are the perfect proportions, providing a secure hold without being cumbersome to the overall design.

Bezel size was not an issue for me, although some people who strive for perfection might discover some tiny flaws in it.

Enjoying one's time spent with the Galaxy Tab is a real treat. It achieves the perfect equilibrium between the amount of screen space available and the overall size. For me, I frequently use tablets to watch movies, television shows, and various other forms of visual media while I am traveling or lying in bed. It was never an inconvenience for me to use this ultra-thin gadget; in fact, I looked forward with great anticipation to taking in media on the Galaxy Tab S9.

Of course, certain differences have emerged, which is to be anticipated given the passage of time and generations. There is only one camera available to us now because one of the rear cameras has been stolen. This one camera features a fresh new design that is streamlined and closely resembles the Galaxy S23 series. The absence of a camera island results in the camera lens having a little protrusion at the back of the device. This modification is quite subtle.

You can magnetically secure the S Pen to the back of the tablet and even use it as a basic kickstand thanks to the magnetic strip that was used to attach the stylus to the tablet in the first place. This strip is located at the rear of the tablet and was used to attach the stylus. The support for charging the S Pen in any orientation is something brand new with this update. Previously, in order to charge the S Pen, you were required to attach it in a particular orientation; now, with the Tab S9, you may attach it in any orientation, and it will charge automatically. That takes care of one annoyance that we had to worry about!

In addition, Samsung has provided each Galaxy Tab S9 tablet with complete protection against dust and water according to the IP68 standard so that users can have peace of mind. Because it has an IP68 designation, the tablet can survive being submerged in water for up to half an hour, however we do not recommend subjecting any electronic device to such harsh conditions.

Graphite and beige are the two color options for the Samsung Galaxy Tab S9, which comes in a variety of sizes. When compared to the Galaxy Tab S8 series, which provided a greater variety of hues, such as graphite, silver, pink, and gold, this feels like a bit of a downgrade in terms of availability.

Display

The revolutionary OLED display of the Galaxy Tab S9 is without a doubt the product highlight, as it possesses unrivaled contrast and colors that are vivid and full of life, in addition to remarkable brightness. Despite the fact that I don't frequently use tablets outside, the remarkable brightness of the display gives me high hopes for the device's visibility in bright settings. Sorry to see you go, LCD, but at least from the point of view of this author, you won't be missed!

Aside from this incredible breakthrough in display technology, the essential screen specs have remained basically intact for the most part. The 11-inch screen keeps its silky smooth refresh rate of 120Hz, making scrolling and multimedia consumption a tremendously enjoyable experience overall. Support for HDR 10+ is also included, which guarantees a superior level of media quality regardless of whether the video being viewed is in HDR or not.

Outstanding colors, amazing contrast, maximum brightness, and commendable viewing angles are all brought to you by the Galaxy Tab S9, which manages to cram all of these features into a form factor that is rather tiny. I've never had any problems with the functionality of the fingerprint sensor that's built into the display; it's both quick and accurate. In addition, there is a practical face unlock feature that allows the tablet to be unlocked even more quickly, but it is possible that this is not the most secure available choice.

Camera

When talking about tablet technology, cameras are sometimes given very little attention because they are frequently seen as an afterthought rather than a big selling element. This trend is continued with the Galaxy Tab S9, which features a single ultra-wide back camera with a modest resolution of 13 megapixels and a front-facing camera with a rating of 12 megapixels.

Main Camera

The merits of the tablet can be summed up in a single sentence thanks to its rear camera, which is a 13-megapixel ultra-wide camera that also has autofocus. In all honesty, it is a decent camera that is capable of completing the task at hand. However, it does not have the same level of complexity as the cameras in flagship phones. It is capable of taking photographs that are, on the whole, passable, despite the fact that the images may contain some noise and lack fine details. The camera has a <u>digital zoom of up to 8.0 times</u>, but I wouldn't recommend utilizing it unless absolutely necessary.

Selfie Camera

[handwritten margin note: comma ? slope]

A 12 megapixel ultra-wide selfie camera is discretely embedded into the <u>bezels</u> on the front of the Galaxy Tab S9. This camera is likely to become more important to you as you go about your day-to-day activities, particularly for video calls and other activities of a similar nature.

The performance of the front camera's HDR mode leaves something to be desired, particularly in challenging situations, just like the performance of the rear camera's HDR mode. The front camera's performance is comparable to that of the rear camera. Additionally, it allows for a zoom of up to 8 times.

In terms of video capabilities, both the front and back cameras are capable of recording films in UHD, FHD, and HD, albeit with a maximum frame rate of 30 frames per second, which prevents the creation of smooth videos at 60 frames per second.

Performance

Since it is powered by the Qualcomm Snapdragon 8 Gen 2 for Galaxy chipset, the Galaxy Tab S9 is a resounding success from every conceivable standpoint. This chipset is truly worthy of being called a flagship performer because of its exceptional energy economy and excellent performance.

It is essentially a polished and slightly overclocked form of the Snapdragon 8 Gen 2 chip that has a speed of 3.32 GHz and can be found in the Galaxy S23 series. Inside the Snapdragon, you'll discover a vapor chamber that has been improved with two-way heat dissipation. This makes it possible for the device to perform at its best for longer periods of time.

The Samsung Galaxy Tab S9 excels in every aspect of its performance. It regularly provides power that appears to have no limits, which transforms the console into an unexpected gaming powerhouse that can easily handle games that require a lot of resources without causing serious overheating concerns. Even while it could get a little toasty when you play for a long time, the temperature is still well within the typical range. The purchase of this tablet ought to be seriously considered by gamers.

The Galaxy Tab S9 boasts impressive features, including 8 gigabytes of random access memory (RAM) and 128 gigabytes of internal storage. On the other hand, if you desire more, you have the option of purchasing the tablet with 12 gigabytes of random access memory (RAM) and 256 gigabytes of storage space. This provides a really flagship-level experience along with adequate space for images, videos, and other types of information.

If I were going to buy this tablet for myself, I would go for the version that has more advanced features. In addition, there is a slot for a microSD card, which enables the storage capacity of your smartphone to be easily expanded. This makes it possible for you to store even more stuff with no difficulty.

It is important to take note that the Samsung Galaxy Tab S9 is not sold in a cellular model and is only offered in a Wi-Fi form.   *modem create wi Fi*

Software

When it comes to its operating system, the Galaxy Tab S9 utilizes Android version 13, which is layered atop Samsung's exclusive One UI 5.1 user interface. It is the culmination of all of Samsung's efforts to personalize their products because it is jam-packed with a wide variety of features and functionality. Notably, it now allows customized lock screens and ? more interface customization, which will bring users who have recently used a Samsung device with One UI back to a familiar experience.

In addition, the introduction of the S Pen gives an additional layer of functionality to the device, making it possible to perform a variety of tasks such as taking notes, capturing creative screenshots, and more. In addition, a number of apps that are not available on other platforms, such as GoodNotes, LumaFusion, Clip Studio Point, and ArcSite, have been developed specifically for use on the Galaxy Tab S9, which increases the tablet's overall usefulness.

It is important to take note of the reintroduction of the potent DeX Mode, which replicates the atmosphere of a laptop computer. It connects without any problems with the new Book Cover Keyboard that is available for the Galaxy Tab S9, which makes it easier to multitask with features such as split-screen and MultiControl.

In terms of long-term support, it is anticipated that the Galaxy Tab S9 will receive four significant Android software updates, which will ensure compatibility up to Android 17. Additionally, Samsung has promised to provide five years of security support, which will bring the total number of years that the gadget will receive security upgrades to 2028. This enhanced support period ensures a lengthy lifespan for this brand-new tablet, which is very amazing.

Battery and Charging

The battery capacity of the Galaxy Tab S9 has been increased by 400mAh in comparison to the battery capacity of its predecessor, the Galaxy Tab S8. This change is understated but very welcomed, and it works in perfect harmony with the Snapdragon 8 Gen 2 for Galaxy chip, which is highly efficient and provides exceptional battery life. This tablet has enough battery life to last through a whole workday even with continuous use. However, it is important to keep in mind that video playback has a tendency to drain the battery a little bit faster when compared to gaming and online surfing; as a result, it is advised to regulate your usage accordingly.

The Galaxy Tab S9 consistently gives battery life statistics that are comparable to those of its competitors when subjected to our exhaustive battery testing. For these tests, we assure a Wi-Fi connection and keep the display brightness at a constant level of 200 nits. It holds its own in a healthy competition with the Google Pixel Tablet and Apple's 11-inch iPad Pro from the previous year. Most notably, the Galaxy Tab S9 came out on top in our gaming test, beating out both of its rivals. Nevertheless, it is not as fast as the iPad in the online surfing test that we conducted, which replicated usual browsing behaviors.

The Galaxy Tab S9 is compatible with charging speeds of up to 45W, which is on par with its predecessor and should fulfill the requirements of the vast majority of users. Because a wall charger is not included in the package, you will either need to purchase one separately or make use of a charging brick that is compatible with your device. This is an important point to keep in mind. The Galaxy Tab S9's battery can be fully recharged in less than an hour and a half when charged with the

Samsung 45W charger, which is a very respectable time frame overall.

Audio quality and haptics

Samsung brags that the speakers in the Galaxy Tab S9 series are 20% larger than those in the prior generation, and it is true that the Galaxy Tab S9 produces a sound that is noticeably louder than its predecessor. On the other hand, I had hoped for a more immersive audio experience with higher clarity, as the sound does not have enough depth, particularly in the lower frequencies. Although it is compatible with Dolby Atmos, and it would appear that the well-known Samsung partner AKG was involved in the development of the quad-speaker system,

Let's move on to the topic of haptics now. The Samsung Galaxy Tab S9 does not, alas, have a flawless performance in every department. In point of fact, it's a long way from being flawless. I don't mind being honest when I say that the haptic feedback on this device is among the worst I've ever experienced in my life. It has the consistency of mush, lacks precision, and is a total letdown. To put this into perspective, I had possessed a Samsung Galaxy Tab S4, which, whether you choose to believe it or not, provided a more satisfying haptic feedback experience.

Alternatives

Samsung is releasing three new tablet versions in addition to the Galaxy Tab S9, namely the Galaxy Tab S9+, the Galaxy Tab S9 Ultra, and the Galaxy Tab S9 Pro. While the Galaxy Tab S9+ is simply an enlarged version of the Galaxy Tab S9, having an additional camera, a larger display, and a more capacious battery, the Galaxy Tab S9 Ultra takes innovation to the extreme with its gigantic 14.6-inch notched screen and top-tier technical specifications. While the Galaxy Tab S9+ is essentially an enlarged version of the Galaxy Tab S9, it also features a larger display.

Rival tablets to the Samsung Galaxy Tab S9

Even if it has an LCD screen that is a little bit antiquated and hardware that is a little bit older, the Galaxy Tab S8's predecessor stands out among the notable competitors in the tablet industry. Those looking for an Android tablet that is less expensive should nevertheless strongly consider purchasing this one.

iPads made by Apple also present a substantial obstacle, as seen by the fact that competing models include the iPad 10th Generation and the most recent iPad Air. However, the iPad Pro (2022) will become the Galaxy Tab S9's most direct competition in the next years. The Google Pixel Tablet has been added to the mix, making for a formidable line-up of devices that are competing against Samsung's most recent offering in the market for tiny tablets for supremacy.

Summary

The Galaxy Tab S9 improves upon its predecessor, the Galaxy Tab S8, by addressing some of that device's faults while also introducing several new capabilities. This sleek and surprisingly potent Android tablet features a display that is sure to take your breath away, and it also comes with a useful S Pen as part of the deal. It has a large amount of storage space, a user interface with a high level of functionality, and powerful multitasking capabilities.

Undoubtedly, there are some rather small downsides associated with it. It would have been nice to have a more powerful sound system, a camera that is just a little bit more advanced, and enhanced haptic feedback. These are, however, somewhat inconsequential problems when viewed in the broader perspective of what elevates a tablet beyond the category of typical electronic devices.

In 2023, everyone who is considering purchasing a tablet should give serious thought to the Galaxy Tab S9 because it is unequivocally a top-tier Android tablet that deserves to be considered. Considering its price of $800, it is possible that it is not the most wallet-friendly alternative; nonetheless, Samsung usually offers several bargains and promotions, making it worthwhile to investigate this portable powerhouse.

CHAPTER TWO

New Features of Samsung Tab S9 plus

In 2023, if you are looking for an Android tablet with a lot of power, it is practically impossible to ignore the new Galaxy Tab S9 Plus. This 12.4-inch powerhouse was launched alongside the Galaxy Z Flip 5, Galaxy Z Fold 5, Galaxy Watch 6, and Galaxy Watch 6 Classic. It fits well between the small Galaxy Tab S9 and the spacious Galaxy Tab S9 Ultra, and it was announced alongside those other products.

Even though the Galaxy Tab S9 Plus has a number of improvements that are noticeable in comparison to its predecessor, the Galaxy Tab S8 Plus, these upgrades are not game-changing in any way. You'll still find the same expansive display and exquisite design on the Galaxy Tab S9, but now it's partnered with the brand-new Snapdragon 8 Gen 2 for Galaxy chip, which not only delivers great performance but also solidifies the device as a real flagship tablet.

When it comes to Samsung's most recent products, I find that the Galaxy Tab S9 Plus is the one that best suits my needs. Although the smaller Galaxy Tab S9 is more portable and simpler to handle (both of which are great benefits for me), the additional screen real estate provided by this model is a feature that is very much appreciated. In addition, the improved performance and extended battery life make this tablet a strong contender for having the greatest value among Samsung's current lineup of Galaxy tablets.

What's new about this device?

internal

Introducing the lightning-fast Snapdragon 8 Gen 2 chipset for the Galaxy, now with:

- Galaxy S23-inspired rear camera design
- IP68 water resistance for added durability
- Included S Pen for enhanced productivity

- Upgraded speakers for a richer audio experience
- Optional cellular connectivity for seamless on-the-go connectivity
- Enhanced 8MP ultra-wide camera for stunning wide-angle shots

Unboxing

The Samsung Galaxy Tab S9 Plus includes minimal accessories in the box. While it doesn't come with a charger, the package includes:

- Galaxy Tab S9 Plus tablet
- S Pen stylus

- USB-C charging cable
- Instruction leaflets and manuals ? not found.

Specs

The most notable improvement is the addition of the Qualcomm Snapdragon 8 Gen 2 for Galaxy, which brings the performance of the Galaxy Tab series up to the level of flagship devices. The remaining hardware parameters are almost an exact replication of those found in the Galaxy Tab S8 Plus.

Dimensions:

- 185.4 x 285.4 x 5.7mm

Weight:

- (Wi-Fi): 581g, (5G): 586g

Operating System (OS):

- Android 13 for all models

Display:

- 12.4-inch Dynamic AMOLED 2X

Refresh Rate:

- All Models: 120Hz

CPU:

- All Models: Snapdragon 8 Gen 2 for Galaxy

RAM:

- 12GB

Storage:

- 256GB, 512GB options

Battery:

- 10,090mAh   / from 8.4

Rear Cameras:

- 13MP main, 8MP ultra-wide

Front Cameras:

- 12MP ultra-wide

Design and Colors

If you've had the opportunity to investigate the Galaxy Tab S8 Plus, you'll find that a significant portion of what makes the Galaxy Tab S9 Plus intriguing is the same as it was in the previous model. The sleek and slimline form factor of the Galaxy Tab S9 Plus completely justifies Samsung's decision to opt for a design continuity policy, which the company has chosen to implement.

This tablet is made from Armor Aluminum, which gives it a sophisticated look while also making it extremely durable. This construction method ensures that the tablet can easily withstand a few scratches and dings. It keeps its 16:10 aspect ratio, which means that it is narrower than an iPad, but it is excellent for providing an immersive experience when watching movies and television shows.

The Samsung Galaxy Tab S9 Plus oozes sophistication with its low profile and side bezels that are exactly proportioned, enabling ergonomic comfort while in use. Its size does not prevent it from remaining very lightweight, which makes it a delight to work with.

When compared to the Tab S9, the Galaxy Tab S9 Plus keeps both of its rear cameras, albeit with a slightly updated design. This is in contrast to the Tab S9. The previous, smaller camera island has been removed and replaced with a new design that is compatible with the Galaxy S23 series. The new design features two cameras that are perfectly integrated into the rear of the tablet.

Since the S Pen has been thoughtfully included in the bundle, you will have no problem getting started on your note-taking right away. An intriguing new feature is the omni-directional magnetic S Pen attachment strip that is located on the back of the device. This strip ensures that charging the S Pen is a hassle-free experience by doing away with the prior fussing that was connected with charging the S Pen.

The complete IP68 dust and water resistance of the Galaxy Tab S9 series is a major improvement that comes with this model. This pill has the potential to tolerate being submerged in liquid for up to half an hour, making it resistant to a wide variety of liquid-related accidents, particularly those involving clean water. However, it is recommended that the IP68 ingress protection rating not be put to its maximum paces during testing.

This year, Samsung has taken a more conservative approach in terms of color options, and the only two colors that will be available for the Galaxy Tab S9 Plus are graphite and beige. When compared to the Graphite, Silver, Pink, and Gold color options that were previously available for the Galaxy Tab S8 Plus, these choices, despite exuding sophistication and understatement, can be considered being a little underwhelming.

Display

You are in luck if you have a preference for displays with a screen size of 12.4 inches that use the Dynamic AMOLED 2X technology and have a refresh rate that ranges from 60 to 120 hertz, feature outstanding brightness, and commendable resolution. These exact parameters characterize the display of the Galaxy Tab S9 Plus, and in my opinion, there is no other information that is necessary or helpful to include.

It is important to note that the Galaxy Tab S9 Plus keeps the same aspect ratio as its predecessor, which is 16:10, giving it a breadth that differentiates it from the design of an iPad, which is slightly more compact. However, this aspect ratio works like a charm for cinematic ventures since it makes the most of the screen's real estate, which results in a panoramic picture that makes the spectator feel as though they are being engulfed by the experience. As we go closer to the end of 2023, the enticing nature of this feature positions the Galaxy Tab S9

Plus as an excellent option for the discriminating cinephile.

When it comes to the real world, the display that the Galaxy Tab S9 Plus offers is nothing short of magnificent. The color rendering is rather impressive, the Vision Booster feature allows for the maximum amount of brightness to be achieved, and the seamless scrolling adds an elegant finishing touch to the process of taking in a wide variety of content. The content comes to life regardless of whether one is actively consuming media or simply browsing for entertainment purposes, and there is no limit to the extent to which one can indulge.

The Galaxy Tab S9 Plus incorporates a fingerprint scanner directly into its display, making it a leader in the field of biometrics. Its speed and accuracy are commendable, and the large recognition area contributes significantly to the ease with which it can be utilized. Even though it is vital to highlight that this method relies on a static image and hence shouldn't be relied upon entirely for security,

Samsung has implemented facial recognition as a convenient extra feature. However, it is crucial to note that this feature was integrated by Samsung as an added convenience.

Camera

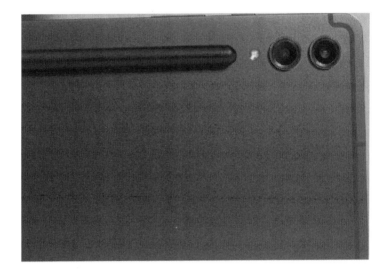

The main camera on the tablet has a resolution of 13 megapixels and is equipped with autofocus. Additionally, the tablet has an ultra-wide camera with a resolution of 8 megapixels, which is an upgrade from the 6 megapixel camera seen on the Galaxy Tab S8 Plus. Nevertheless, as is the case with the vast majority of tablets, the cameras appear to be a secondary consideration. Despite the fact that Samsung has not introduced any substantial new features to this essential component, this is still one of the most important aspects of the device.

The Main Camera:

At best, the performance of the primary camera can be described as adequate. Although it takes photographs that are passable, they do not have the same vividness or sharpness as those produced by dedicated cameras. Additionally, there can be some background noise in the images. When taking photographs using a tablet, it is essential to have reasonable expectations in order to avoid being disappointed.

Ultra Wide-Camera:

The ultra-wide camera performs similarly to the primary camera in that it offers a more expansive field of view. However, in terms of image quality, the ultra-wide camera does not considerably outperform the primary camera.

Selfie Camera:

On the front of the device is a single ultra-wide camera with 12 megapixels. This camera is perhaps more important than the rear camera because it is the one that will be used for video chats and business meetings on services such as Zoom and Teams. Selfies captured with this camera are usable, but they frequently lack fine details and may have noise difficulties. The camera also has several other limitations. Again, it is essential to keep in mind that tablets are not often designed to perform at the same level as high-end cameras in terms of photography.

Performance

The most recent Qualcomm Snapdragon 8 Gen 2 for Galaxy chipset is featured in the Galaxy Tab S9 Plus, which is designed to be comparable to the Galaxy S23 series. The highest clock rate of this variant is 3.36 gigahertz, which is significantly higher than the typical 3.2 gigahertz that is found in the

Snapdragon 8 Gen 2 chip. This variant also offers a few other minor improvements over the base model. It contains a novel vapor chamber that has two-way heat dissipation, which allows the device to retain peak performance for extended periods of time. This is done to ensure that the thermal performance is at its optimum.

There is no doubt about it: the performance of this chipset is unparalleled, as is the quality of the gaming experience it provides. Gamers who are looking forward to Samsung's upcoming mid-sized tablet will be excited to hear that the Snapdragon 8 Gen 2 CPU competes with Apple's latest A16 Bionic chip in terms of graphics processing. This will make the Snapdragon 8 Gen 2 a welcome addition. The responsiveness of the tablet is very astounding, making a multitude of opportunities readily available at your disposal.

The Galaxy Tab S9 Plus comes in two different storage capacities, 256 gigabytes and 512 gigabytes, and features a total of 12 gigabytes of

LPDDR5X RAM. It's important to note that Samsung has kept the microSD card slot, which gives consumers the opportunity to easily add more storage space to their devices.

Galaxy Tab S9 Plus Cellular Connectivity

A notable feature of the Galaxy Tab S9 Plus is its cellular connectivity, setting it apart from the other new Galaxy tablets. Surprisingly, even the high-end Galaxy Tab S9 Ultra doesn't offer optional cellular connectivity, which is quite unusual.

The Galaxy Tab S9 Plus is available with 5G support through AT&T, US Cellular, or Verizon. It's important to note, however, that when opting for cellular connectivity, your storage and memory options are limited to 12GB of RAM and 256GB of storage. Unfortunately, the 512GB version is not available in this configuration.

Software

Android 13 is the operating system that makes its debut on the Galaxy Tab S9 Plus, and Samsung's sophisticated One UI 5.1 interface is placed on top of that. In addition to the standard Android user experience, Samsung's customized user interface shines in its prime form, offering a variety of features and functionalities that distinguish it from its rivals in a significant way.

Users of this tablet will have the ability to scribble down notes, unleash their creativity through drawing, and capture imaginative screenshots thanks to the inclusion of the S Pen. Samsung has introduced a variety of intriguing apps that have been exclusively crafted for the Galaxy Tab series. These apps, which were once limited to iOS, include GoodNotes, LumaFusion, Clip Studio Point, and ArcSite. These apps add to the attractiveness of the Galaxy Tab series. Notably, GoodNotes will initially only be available for use on Galaxy Tab devices when it launches for Android.

The user-favorite DeX Mode environment, which imitates a PC-like setup, and the Multi Window function both make a victorious comeback, further enhancing the usefulness of the Galaxy Tab S9 Plus. Both of these capabilities are renowned for their ability to reproduce a PC-like environment.

Samsung is dedicated to enhancing the user experience of the Galaxy Tab S9 Plus, and the company has pledged to deliver four major Android updates in addition to five years' worth of critical bug fixes. This comprehensive support guarantees that the tablet will continue to be supported by Android 14, Android 15, Android 16, and even Android 17, ensuring that it has a lengthy lifespan. You can rest easy knowing that this system will continue to be protected from newly discovered vulnerabilities until the year 2028.

Battery and Charging

With the Galaxy Tab S9 Plus, Samsung maintains its practice of include a battery that is the same size as the one found in the Tab S8 Plus, which was the device's predecessor. This generation of the tablet features a battery with a capacity of 10,090 mAh, which, when combined with the newly incorporated processor, greatly increases the operational duration of the device.

In our in-house battery tests, in which the displays of both devices are consistently set to 200 nits of brightness and evaluations are performed while connected to a Wi-Fi network, the Galaxy Tab S9 Plus demonstrates superior longevity in comparison to its smaller counterpart, the Galaxy Tab S9. This difference is especially noticeable in our tests for web browsing and 3D gaming. It performs brilliantly in the endurance competition.

On the other hand, it does not do as well as the Pixel Tablet in the video streaming benchmark. This is partly because the Pixel Tablet has an LCD screen that consumes less power. Despite this, the Galaxy Tab S9 Plus shines brightest in both our tests of online browsing and 3D gaming. When it comes to tablets,

I think the Galaxy Tab S9 Plus is a better option than the Google Pixel Tablet.

From my own experience with the Galaxy Tab S9 Plus, I can confidently say that its battery life can easily last through a full day of usage, which includes a variety of media-focused activities. It is vital to keep in mind that the tablet's battery will drain much more quickly if you watch videos with the brightness turned up to its maximum setting, despite the fact that it is a natural and understandable impulse. If keeping up with your media consumption is one of your top priorities, positioning a charging solution nearby is a smart idea.

The Galaxy Tab S9 Plus maintains compatibility for 45W charging speeds, just like its predecessor was able to do. This feature was introduced with the Galaxy Tab S8 Plus. This makes it possible to charge rates that are better than satisfactory. It takes about two hours to get a full charge, which is on the longer side compared to other charging times. It is important to note that the box does not come with a charger; therefore, you will need to provide your own charging equipment in order to utilize the product.

Audio quality and haptics

The Galaxy Tab S9 series, including the Galaxy Tab S9 Plus, all come equipped with speakers that are enlarged by 20% thanks to a decision made by Samsung. These speakers have complete compatibility for Dolby Atmos and have been fine-tuned by AKG, which is a partner company of Samsung. Despite the fact that these larger speakers produce a louder sound, they are lacking in the lower frequencies, which results in a sound that is rather metallic and reminiscent of a tablet. It should be made clear that the consumption of media on the gadget is still a pleasurable experience; yet, there was hope for an even more robust and immersive auditory experience.

A mediocre haptic feedback vibrator motor is present in the Galaxy Tab S9 Plus, just as it is in its smaller sibling, the Galaxy Tab S9. It has a sluggish operation, is lacking in precision, and generates vibrations that are unclear. Despite the fact that the intensity of the tablet's vibrations can be adjusted, there is no setting that can save this unsatisfactory feature of the device. In the end, I discovered that completely disabling the haptic feedback was the most efficient course of action to take. To improve this facet of the user experience, Samsung ought to think about incorporating Apple's haptic feedback technology into its upcoming tablets.using your own personal charging apparatus.

Alternatives

The Galaxy Tab S9 Plus is making a sizeable expansion across many devices, the majority of which are manufactured by Samsung. This is an important development.

iPads, in their various forms, stand out among its competitors; nevertheless, the iPad Pro 12.9-inch model is the primary contender in this race. Importantly, this Pro edition is compatible with the Apple Pencil, and it also comes with the option of purchasing an additional Magic Keyboard accessory. It also has a screen that is marginally larger than the one on the standard iPad, and it has a display that is capable of a respectable 120Hz mini-LED display. It is clearly a significant rival that deserves to be taken into consideration.

The iPad Air of the 5th generation, which is equipped with the robust M1 chip, represents yet another possible competitor. On the other hand, Samsung's earlier Galaxy tablets, like the Galaxy Tab S8 Plus and the Galaxy Tab S7 Plus, also have this capability. Both of these older models remain highly capable of handling a broad variety of tasks, including all of your media and productivity needs, despite the fact that they may not contain the most recent technology.

Last but not least, there's Google's interesting Pixel Tablet, which is not just a tablet but also a smart monitor with a variety of functions. It has a longer overall endurance than the Galaxy Tab S9 Plus when it comes to streaming videos. Nevertheless, it is essential to keep in mind that the Galaxy Tab S9 Plus is still a noticeably more premium gadget, while having a significantly higher price tag.

Summary

The Galaxy Tab S9 Plus is an example of Samsung's established tablet line being improved in a way that is both understated and effective. This is in no way a disadvantage, considering that earlier incarnations of the Galaxy Tab Plus had already reached the highest possible level of performance. Therefore, even relatively insignificant alterations really do make a big difference.

My passion for the Galaxy Tab S9, which is smaller and more portable, has grown over the past year, despite the fact that I have always enjoyed the

Galaxy tablet with a size in the middle. Within its more manageable compact aspect, it maintains the same outstanding hardware and gorgeous display as its predecessor. To clear things up, the Galaxy Tab S9 Plus is in no way a subpar piece of technology; rather, it just provides a screen that is marginally larger at a price that is marginally more. It is so difficult to rationalize purchasing it rather than the Galaxy Tab S9, which is smaller and more reasonably priced.

CHAPTER THREE

New Features of Samsung Tab S9 Ultra

Following up on the trio of Galaxy Tab S8 models it released last year with another trio of Galaxy Tab S9 units, Samsung has shown that it is committed to competing in the premium tablet market. The Samsung Galaxy Tab S9 Ultra is now the largest, most powerful, and most elegant Android tablet that can be purchased. As a result, it is currently in the lead among its competitors.

It comes with a S Pen straight out of the box, it has a screen that's 14.6 inches in size, and it has a quad speaker configuration, so it's safe to say that it's loaded with features. On the other hand, it doesn't diverge too much from its predecessor, the Galaxy Tab S8 Ultra. Is it really necessary to make the upgrade?

After performing a thorough evaluation of the Galaxy Tab S9 Ultra, we will deliver a response that is as complete as possible. In the meanwhile, we have spent some limited hands-on time with the device, and the following are some initial thoughts that we have about it:

What's new about this device?

What's Exciting in the Galaxy Tab S9 Ultra?

- **Powerful Processor**: Equipped with the cutting-edge Snapdragon 8 Gen 2 processor, tailor-made for Galaxy devices.
- **Swift Storage**: Experience faster data access with an upgrade to UFS 4.0, coupled with the efficiency of LPDDR5X RAM.
- **Enhanced Cooling**: Stay cool even during intense tasks, thanks to the internal vapor chamber for advanced thermal management.
- **All-Weather Durability:** Enjoy peace of mind with IP68-rated water and dust resistance, making it ready for any environment.

Specs

The Galaxy Tab S9 Ultra keeps its familiar appearance on the outside, but as the proverb says, "real transformation happens beneath the surface." This is true of the Galaxy Tab S9 Ultra. With this in mind, the Galaxy Tab S9 series reclaims its position at the summit of Android tablets with advancements like as an improved processor and quicker memory chips. These are just two of the many new features that come with this series. In the meantime, the other characteristics are identical to those seen in earlier iterations.

Dimensions:

- 208.6 x 326.4 x 5.5mm

Weight:

- (Wi-Fi): 732g, (5G): 737g

Operating System (OS):

- Android 13 for all models

Display:

- 14.6-inch Dynamic AMOLED 2X

Refresh Rate:

- All Models: 120Hz

CPU:

- All Models: Snapdragon 8 Gen 2 for Galaxy

RAM:

- 12GB, 16GB options

Storage:

- 256GB, 512GB, 1TB options

Battery:

- 11,200mAh

Rear Cameras:

- 13MP main, 8MP ultra-wide

Front Cameras:

- 12MP main, 12MP ultra-wide

Design and Colors

As a result of its imposing dimensions, the Galaxy Tab S8 Ultra made quite an impression on consumers, which raised concerns about the demand for this product in the market. Despite this, it would appear that Samsung is pleased with the performance of the Tab S8 Ultra because the successor, the Tab S9 Ultra, has kept its enormous proportions.

Once again, the design of the Tab S9 Ultra is elegant and wide, and it has low bezels around the screen. In spite of its magnitude, it has the sensation of being relatively light, and it can be held in one hand without too much difficulty. However, because the bezels are so thin, using it when you're moving around can be a bit of a challenge. This is because the thin bezels make it more likely that you'll accidentally touch the display along its edges. This tablet is definitely doable, however it works best for activities that need you to remain still.

The choice between the two color options that are available to you, Beige and Graphite, is a simple one to make because there are only two of each.

In keeping with recent developments, a fingerprint scanner has been incorporated underneath the screen of the device. The well-established nature of Samsung's competence in this field enables the company to provide authentication that is prompt, accurate, and responsive.

Display

A stunning AMOLED display that is 14.6 inches in size demands your admiration. It is a complete AMOLED panel, which has a clear resolution of 2960 x 1848 pixels and full support for HDR10, and it oozes vibrancy, brilliance, and beauty in its purest form.

In addition, it has a refresh rate of 120 Hz, which not only improves the visual experience while scrolling but also provides an excellent tactile sense when using the S Pen. This is a major selling point for the device. Writing and drawing with our S Pen is a very responsive and pleasurable experience since the lines appear to dance to the rhythm of the twists and turns that are created by the S Pen.

Camera

Tablets typically do not place a high priority on their rear-facing cameras because it is not typical for users to utilize a large 14.6-inch tablet as their primary camera, attempting to record a variety of angles while squeezing it into tiny spaces.

The ultra-wide camera on the rear of the Galaxy Tab S9 Ultra has been given a modest upgrade with the introduction of an 8 megapixel sensor, which is an improvement over the previous 6 megapixel sensor. Despite this, the primary camera on the back of the device still has a resolution of 13 megapixels. During the course of our testing, we will take a few photographs with the Samsung Galaxy Tab S9 Ultra. At this stage, it appears that the performance of its camera continues to be roughly comparable to that of the Tab S8 Ultra from the previous year.

Nevertheless, the cameras that face forward are the ones that are most important, particularly for video chats and conferences. There are two 12 megapixel cameras built into this tablet, one of which has a wide-angle lens, and the other of which has an ultra-wide-angle lens.

Performance

The Snapdragon 8 Gen 2 "Made for Galaxy" is the prominent component that can be found in this year's premium Galaxy handsets. This chip was developed by Qualcomm specifically for use in Galaxy products. In essence, it is a version of the flagship CPU that has had its clock speed increased, and it is now capable of achieving rates of up to 3.36 GHz, up from the previous speed of 3.2 GHz.

Samsung has added a new vapor chamber to the Galaxy Tab S9 line of tablets in order to boost the cooling capabilities of the devices. This new information makes the recently released tablets the obvious product of choice for mobile gamers, as it guarantees that the ultra-fast processor will continue to operate at its full performance for a lengthy period of time. The possibility that the CPU will be able to keep its maximum speed for longer intervals of time is very encouraging, and we are looking forward to putting it through our extensive battery of stress testing as soon as possible.

The migration to storage using UFS 4.0 is yet another important improvement that was made under the hood. This shift is noteworthy since the new storage chips offer twice the read and write speeds of their predecessors while simultaneously consuming around 45% less energy overall. In addition, the LPDDR5X RAM has been improved, making it marginally faster than its predecessor. This helps to contribute to a more fluid and consistent experience overall.

Software

One UI 5.0 is the current generation of Samsung's customized version of Android, which is known as One UI. One UI 5.0 is the most recent version. It is a considerable change from the experience of using standard Android, bringing with it a new visual and functional revamp of the OS. This is a significant difference. You will discover the traditional quick toggles in the notification shade of One UI 5.0, as well as persistent app docks and a favorite apps drawer that is positioned to the side of the screen for your convenience. In addition to this, it supports floating applications and provides a simple method for multitasking via split screens.

The capability of Samsung's tablets to activate DeX mode on their own, without the requirement for an external screen connection, is one of the brand's most distinguishing characteristics. Through the use of the DeX mode, your tablet will take on the appearance of a laptop or desktop computer's user interface. Even though it is still Android on the inside, the entire user interface has been redone to look like a desktop environment. This includes an app-filled desktop, a start menu, a taskbar, and a number of other features.

It is significant that Samsung has made a commitment to providing software upgrades and security patches. They guarantee that major Android updates will be released for up to four years, and that security patches would be supported for up to five years. The following is a list of the software upgrades that you may anticipate upon the release of the Galaxy Tab S9 Ultra in the month of August:

- Android 13 will make its debut on the Tab S9 Ultra in 2023.
- Late in the year 2023, an update to Android 14 is released for the Tab S9 Ultra.
- In the late year 2024, the Tab S9 Ultra is upgraded to Android 15.
- In the late year 2025, the Tab S9 Ultra will have evolved into Android 16.

- In the latter part of 2026, the Tab S9 Ultra will upgrade to Android 17.
- Around the middle of the year 2027, the promise of updates will come to an end.
- Around the middle of the year 2028, the last of the security patches will be deployed, signaling the end of official support.

Battery and Charging

The battery on the Galaxy Tab S9 Ultra, just like the battery on the Galaxy Tab S8 Ultra, has an excellent 11,200 mAh capacity, which supplies a large amount of power and should keep you going for an extended period of time. How well the equipment is optimized will determine how long the actual duration will be. We have high hopes that we will see an improvement in efficiency as a result of the implementation of new memory chips and an enhanced Snapdragon CPU. Keep an eye out for the benchmark testing as soon as we get the chance to put the unit to the test.

When it comes to charging the battery, you should probably think about utilizing a charger that is 45 W in order to get the most out of the process. However, I would like to bring to your attention that the box does not contain one of the items.

Audio quality and haptics

The Galaxy Tab line of tablets is equipped with four speakers that are laid out in a stereo format. These four speakers provide a distinct left and right channel audio experience whenever you use the device in either landscape or portrait mode. This is true regardless of which orientation you are using the device in.

The Galaxy Tab Ultra, in particular, takes use of a considerable amount of room for sound to resonate, which leads to robust audio output that is distinguished by rich, low-frequency bass and high frequencies that are remarkably clear. During the hands-on session, we couldn't help but share our excitement over the sound quality of the tablet by playing music. This left an indelible effect on others who were in the room with us.

Alternatives

The iPad Pro 12.9 from Apple is undeniably the most formidable competitor in this sector. Even if it hasn't received an upgrade since 2022, Cupertino's hefty tablet is still in a strong place in the market. It comes equipped with an Apple M2 CPU and an improved Apple Pencil that supports hover capability, despite the fact that this feature has been available on Galaxy Tabs for years.

Both the iPad and the Samsung Galaxy Tab have access to high-quality keyboard attachments and styluses (the Samsung Galaxy Tab even comes with a stylus in the box), so the choice you make will likely come down to which environment you prefer.

LumaFusion is a video editor, and Samsung has helped facilitate its migration to the Android platform, which has contributed to the increased competitiveness of the Galaxy Tab. On the other hand, Apple quickly responded by introducing Final Cut Pro and Logic Pro on iPads, which was a long overdue development.

Summary

There is no question that Samsung's most recent premium tablet packs quite a punch. Although it comes with a large price tag, Samsung makes the purchase more enticing by offering pre-order customers complimentary storage upgrades as well as an improved trade-in promotion program.

Is there a return on the money spent on it? That, of course, is dependant on the application you have in mind. We are not simply referring to mindless activities such as binge-watching on Netflix or scrolling on Instagram. Because of its capabilities with DeX, the Galaxy Tab S9 Ultra is a flexible tool that can be used for a variety of tasks, including drawing, editing, and even managing text documents and spreadsheets. If you use a tablet frequently and extensively for work on a regular basis, it is likely to result in an increase in your overall level of productivity over time. Given the circumstances, the cost might be understood as a strategic investment instead.

However, the tablet's form factor is something that causes us to have some reservations about it. The portability of tablets is the primary selling point for these devices. The Tab Ultra variants, on the other hand, have dimensions that are rather considerable and are practically identical to those of laptops, despite being thinner and less heavy. If you attach a keyboard to one of these devices, it essentially transforms it into a laptop. Therefore, the question that emerges is whether you should splurge on a luxury tablet or whether you should instead go with a premium laptop.

Do you currently have a Tab S8 Ultra in your possession? How would you describe the results of using it? Or have you ever thought about making use of one in the future?

CHAPTER FOUR

Set up your device

You have recently purchased a brand new Samsung Galaxy tablet, and you are probably curious about how to get things started with it. The first thing you need to do is use Smart Switch, which will make the process of transferring data from your prior tablet or even a phone very simple for you. If you have a preference for a wired or wireless means of file transfer, or if you'd like to use an external storage device such as a microSD card, Smart Switch can accommodate your requirements.

If you are migrating from an iOS device, you can use iCloud in conjunction with Smart Switch to transfer all of your data in an easy and seamless manner. Rest assured, Smart Switch also offers robust security options to ensure the safety of your data during the transfer process, so you can make the transition to your new tablet with peace of mind.

How to turn on your Tab S9 Series for the First time

There is a possibility that the procedure of setting up your tablet will change depending on whether it connects to the internet by Wi-Fi or LTE as well. Let's assume that these steps do not perfectly coincide with the settings of your tablet, or in the event that you require assistance with setting up a SIM card, you should think about consulting your carrier for particular instructions.

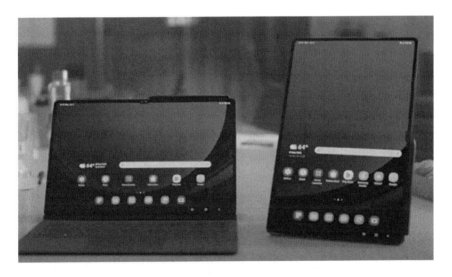

- **Power on your tablet**. After it has finished going through its starting routine, you will be presented with the Welcome page, where you will be able to select the language that you would want to use. To continue, tap the "Start" button.

- **Take** a moment while you go over the Terms and Conditions, Privacy Policy, and the options available for the sharing of diagnostic data. After that, you need to press "Agree to All" followed by "Agree" to proceed.

- The instructions may differ somewhat for tablets that are LTE-enabled at this point. Let's say that you must install and activate a SIM card, it is recommended that you get in touch with your carrier in order to guarantee that the activation procedure is completed correctly. You can skip this step if your tablet does not support LTE or if you do not intend to use a SIM card to connect to the internet.

- Choose a Wi-Fi network to connect to. Establishing a Wi-Fi connection is necessary if you want to get the most out of the capabilities of your tablet. Your tablet will look for available networks; all you have to do is select the one you want to use. In the event that your network is concealed, choose "Add network" and key in the information by hand. To connect, you will need to enter the password for the network.

- Your tablet will require a few minutes of your time after it has successfully connected to the network of your choice in order to establish the settings that you have just selected. After this, you will be given the option to move apps and data from an older smartphone to the new one. Proceed to the part that is titled "Ways to transfer your content." Choose the "Don't copy" option if you'd rather not move any of the data from one device to another. You are required to have both a Google Account and a Samsung Account in order to use the tablet to its full potential. From this point on, you will be walked through the steps of creating a Google Account and a Samsung Account. To finish these tasks, follow the directions that appear on the screen.

Ways to transfer your content

Before moving forward, you will need to decide which of the several methods for transferring data via Smart Switch is your top choice. The following information provides an overview of the various possibilities that are open to you: transferring data wirelessly, transferring data by USB cable, transferring data using iCloud, and transferring data using an external storage device.

- **Wireless transfer:** Transferring content from one device to another can be accomplished in a short amount of time using this technology, which is known as wireless transfer. You have the option of keeping your devices connected to a power source throughout the transfer, which will prevent the battery from being damaged in any way.

Before beginning the transfer, it is necessary to ensure that both devices have the Smart Switch application loaded.

- **Transfer Using a USB connection**: You can connect your devices using a USB connection in order to do a transfer that is both more secure and more dependable. Be aware, however, that you won't be able to charge both of your devices at the same time; therefore, you should make sure that both of your devices have a full charge before beginning the transfer.

- **Transferring via iCloud**: If you're moving from an iPhone, Smart Switch will be able to access any data that was previously stored in iCloud. Before you start the transfer, you should check your iPhone once more to make sure that all the important data has been backed up to iCloud. This is a precaution you should take in case any of the data is lost.

- **Transferring Your information Using an External Device**: Making use of an external storage device is yet another potential alternative available to you when it comes to transferring your information. You can create a backup of your data on one device using a microSD card or a USB OTG flash drive, and then transfer that backup to another device. In order to accomplish this, you will first need to generate a backup of your data by inserting the flash drive or microSD card into your previous device. Only then can you move on to the next step in the transfer process.

Content that can and cannot be

transferred with Smart Switch

While Smart Switch offers a versatile range of data transfer options, encompassing contacts, call history, call logs, photos, videos, and documents, it's essential to be aware of certain data types that aren't supported by the application. For a comprehensive understanding of which file formats require individual transfer methods, please consult the following information:

Also note that content synchronized with external services, such as calendars linked to Office or Google, cannot be transferred via Smart Switch. However, you can easily synchronize such data by adding the respective account to your new device.

Data Transferable from Android:

While Smart Switch offers a versatile range of data transfer options, encompassing contacts, call history, call logs, photos, videos, and documents, it's essential to be aware of certain data types that aren't supported by the application. For a comprehensive understanding of which file formats require individual transfer methods, please consult the following information:

Also note that content synchronized with external services, such as calendars linked to Office or Google, cannot be transferred via Smart Switch.

However, you can easily synchronize such data by adding the respective account to your new device.

Data Transferable from Android:

- **Personal Content:** Contacts, S Planner, Messages, Memo, Call logs, Clock, and Internet.
- **App Data:** Images, Music (DRM-free content only), Videos (DRM-free content only), Documents, Story Album, and Applications.

  Photos
- **Settings, etc.:** Email, Wallpaper, Lock screen, Radio, and Preferences.

Data Transferable from iOS via iCloud:

- **Personal Content:** Contacts, Schedule, Notes, Call history, and Bookmarks.
- **App Data**: Photos, Videos (DRM-free content only), Documents, Recommended apps, and Voice Memos.
- **Settings, etc.:** Wi-Fi and Alarms.

Data Transferable via USB Cable:

- **Personal Content:** Contacts, Schedule, Messages, Notes, Call history, and Bookmarks.
- **App Data:** Photos, Music (DRM-free content only), Videos (DRM-free content only), Documents, Recommended apps, and Voice Memos.
- **Settings, etc.:** Wi-Fi and Alarms.

This information should help you effectively manage your data transfer requirements, ensuring a smooth transition to your new device.

- **Personal Content:** Contacts, S Planner, Messages, Memo, Call logs, Clock, and Internet.
- **App Data:** Images, Music (DRM-free content only), Videos (DRM-free content only), Documents, Story Album, and Applications.
- **Settings, etc.:** Email, Wallpaper, Lock screen, Radio, and Preferences.

Data Transferable from iOS via iCloud:

- **Personal Content**: Contacts, Schedule, Notes, Call history, and Bookmarks.
- **App Data:** Photos, Videos (DRM-free content only), Documents, Recommended apps, and Voice Memos.
- **Settings, etc.:** Wi-Fi and Alarms.

Data Transferable via USB Cable:

- **Personal Content**: Contacts, Schedule, Messages, Notes, Call history, and Bookmarks.
- **App Data:** Photos, Music (DRM-free content only), Videos (DRM-free content only), Documents, Recommended apps, and Voice Memos.
- **Settings, etc.:** Wi-Fi and Alarms.

This information should help you effectively manage your data transfer requirements, ensuring a smooth transition to your new device.

Smart Switch Settings

There is a possibility that you are concerned about the safety of your content while it is being transferred. Thankfully, Smart Switch has a number of different security mechanisms that may be utilized by you in order to keep your data safe. You have the opportunity to enable these settings in order to set authentication and password prerequisites for data transfers. These requirements must be met before any data can be transferred.

To access these security settings, simply do the following:

- Launch the **Smart Switch application** on your device.
- To access further customization options, select the icon depicted by three stacked dots.
- Make sure you select "Settings."
- Pick the method of protection that best meets your requirements.

The following are the various precautionary measures that can be taken:

- **Enhance Transfer Security:** This is a feature that, when enabled, requires users to enter an authentication number before commencing file transfers. This provides an additional layer of safety for the data you are transferring.

- **Encryption of External Storage:** When recovering backup files from external storage devices like microSD cards and USB storage devices, you have the option to select the type of encryption that best suits your needs. This helps to keep your data private.

- **Encryption for Secure Folders:** In a similar vein, when restoring backup files from Secure Folder, you have the option of selecting the encryption method that best suits your needs, thereby preserving the confidentiality of your files.

In addition, you may obtain information about the software version by tapping on the "About Smart

Switch" button. Here, you can check the Terms of Service and investigate the open-source license in further depth. It is essential to maintain the most recent version of Smart Switch by constantly updating it to the most recent release. This will guarantee that you benefit from the most recent security patches and features.

CHAPTER FIVE

Changing Wallpapers and icons

Your Samsung Tab S9 offers a theme that caters to every individual taste, from those who are passionate about sports to those who appreciate a refined aesthetic. Since you can customize Galaxy themes, Samsung wallpapers, and icons, you can make your smartphone seem exactly the way you want it to in order to make it a perfect fit for your preferences. In addition, these themes can extend their impact to the color schemes of vital elements such as Contacts, Messages, Settings, and the Quick settings panel. This helps to ensure that your device becomes a real expression of your own taste by changing the color schemes of these essential parts.

If you have a Samsung account, you'll have the added benefit of being able to quickly access themes and icons that you've purchased for one of your other devices in the past. Explore the wide variety of phone cases and tablet covers that are available on our website to finish the process of giving your gadget the ideal personalized appearance. Your Galaxy device is more than just a tool; it's an extension of who you are and how you choose to present yourself to the world.

How to download themes

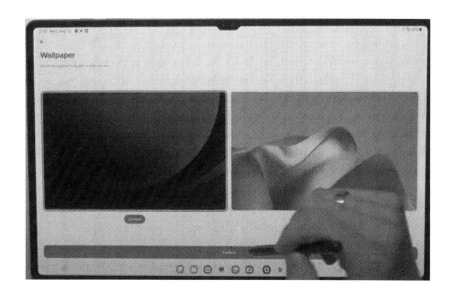

Your Samsung Tab S9 Series can be made more unique by using a theme, which gives you the ability to alter everything from the wallpaper and icons to the default applications, such as Phone, Messages, and Calendar, so that they represent your own particular taste.

Follow these procedures to gain access to the Themes:

- You can access the **Themes menu** by selecting an empty spot on your Home

81

screen, pressing and holding on it, and then selecting "Themes."

- If this is your first time using Themes, take a few moments to read the information that has been provided, and then press "Continue" or "Agree" to move forward with the process.

- Swipe up to explore the different themes that are offered, and choose the one that most appeals to you from the options.

- You can browse through the available themes by visiting the Galaxy Themes Store. If the theme is available for free, all you need to do is tap "Download." Tap on the pricing (for example, $0.99) to see if it is a paid theme.

- You are going to be given the choice to either "Select payment method" or "Use discounts." If it's required, put your payment information here.

- Simply tap the "Pay now" button to finish the purchase.

- You have the option to "Download trial" a premium theme before making a purchase decision if you would want to test it out first. It is important to keep in mind that the only way for you to update a theme is if the person who sold you the theme or the person who created the theme has released an updated version.

Themes also allow you to customize your gadget to reflect your personal taste.

How to change your theme

You have been returning to that theme for a considerable amount of time. If you currently have another one downloaded or saved and you want to change it, the method is straightforward:

- You can access the Themes menu by selecting an empty spot on your Home screen, pressing and holding on it, and then selecting "Themes."
- To view all of your available themes, click the button that looks like three horizontal lines (it's

called the Menu icon), then go to "My stuff," and finally select "Themes."

- Select the theme that you want to use, look through the specifics of it, and then touch "Apply."

- If it's required, you can validate your selection by hitting "Apply" once more.

Note: Be advised that once a theme has been applied, it cannot be removed or changed in any way. Repeat these steps if you want to choose a different theme or revert to the one that was installed by default.

How to download icons

Are you looking for a way to convey your excitement about your favorite pastime? You can give your Samsung tab S9 a more individualized look by installing fresh icons on it.

- To change the look of your device's interface, start from the Home screen, press and hold an empty area, and then pick "Themes."

- To view the many icon sets that are available, navigate to the "Icons" section, and then swipe upwards on the screen. Select the alternative that most piques your curiosity.

- On the Galaxy Themes page, with the "Icons" tab chosen, press "Download" for free icon sets or the specified price (for example, $0.99) for paid ones. Alternatively, you can select a different tab to view premium icon sets.

- You are going to be presented with the option to "Select payment method" or "Use discounts." If this is your first time using Themes, simply take a few moments to read the information that has been provided, and then select "Continue."

- Tap the "Pay now" button to validate your selection.

It is important to take note that icon sets do not have the ability to change all of your app icons, and you cannot use your own images as icons.

How to change icons

It's possible that you're becoming tired of looking at the same icons all the time. If you've previously downloaded or saved another set of icons and you're aching for a change, you may give your interface a new look by following these steps:

- To do this, navigate to the Home screen on your device and tap and hold on an empty place.
- To view the themes, click on "Themes."
- Click the Menu icon, which is typically depicted as three horizontal lines, to access all the icons that are currently available to you. After that, get to "Icons" by clicking "My stuff" first.
- Choose the icon pack that appeals to you the most, and then select "Apply."
- If it's essential, make sure that your selection is correct by hitting "Apply" once more.

Also, remember this approach might not result in changes to the icons of all apps because certain apps have icons that cannot be changed. It is important to keep in mind that the use of your own photos as icons is not supported.

How to delete themes

It appears that you downloaded the wrong theme by accident. Don't be concerned; getting rid of it won't be difficult at all:

- Begin by going to the Home screen on your device.
- Tap and hold anywhere on the screen that is not being used.
- After that, choose "Themes" from the list of available options in the menu that just appeared.
- Find the icon that looks like three horizontal lines and tap it. This symbol is commonly called **the Menu.**

- Select "Purchased items" from the list of available options on the menu.
- You will see a list of the themes you have obtained in this section. Tap the trash can icon (Delete) in the upper right corner of the screen to get rid of the theme (or themes) you no longer want.
- Choose the individual theme or themes that you want to remove from your website.
- To validate your choice, touch the "Delete" button located at the very bottom of the screen.

The unwelcome topic ought to be eliminated without any further difficulty as a result of this action.

How to delete icons

The following procedures need to be taken in order to remove icons:

- You can access the Themes menu by selecting an empty spot on your Home screen, pressing and holding on it, and then selecting "Themes."

- To access the menu, select the button depicted by three lines running horizontally.
- Select "Purchased items," and after that, "Icons."
- Tap the Delete option, which is represented as a trash can icon, located in the upper right corner of the screen. At this point, select the icons that you want to remove.
- Tap the "Delete" button in the bottom-right corner to validate your choices.

If you make a decision that you later regret, you are free to erase any icons that you have added.

How to recover purchased themes

Nobody wants to spend their money more than once on the same thing. If you link your Samsung Tab S9 series to a Samsung account, you will be able to simply restore previously purchased themes, even if you initially got them on a separate device.

This is because you will be able to access your account from any device that is linked to your Samsung account.

This is the procedure to follow:

- You can access the Themes menu by selecting an empty spot on your Home screen, pressing and holding on it, and then selecting "Themes."
- To access the menu, use the icon that looks like three horizontal lines and is located in the top-left corner of the screen.
- Make your selection under "Purchased items."
- Find the theme you want to restore on your device, and then select "Download." You can carry out the steps again and again as many times as is required.

Note: If you use the menu at the top of the screen, you may also use this page to restore previously purchased wallpapers or icons.

How to use color palette options

Your device has a useful feature that enables you to either synchronize the color palette with the wallpaper that is now active on your screen or select colors of your own choosing. Accessing and making use of this functionality can be accomplished as follows:

- Open the "Wallpaper and Style" section of your device's settings by going to "Settings" on your Samsung Tab s9 series.

- To use the color palette, first select "Color Palette" from the menu, and then enable it by toggling the switch that is located next to "Color Palette."

- Choose a color scheme that you like most and that corresponds to your existing wallpaper by clicking on the "Wallpaper Colors" tab. You also have the option of selecting a solid color by tapping the "Basic Colors" button. Swipe left to see further settings options.

- You can get an idea of how the palette you chose will look thanks to the previews that are displayed at the top of the screen.

- Tap the "Apply" button once you've made a decision that satisfies you. This will apply the color palette that you have chosen for all the menus and screens on your device. In addition, you have the choice to turn on the switch that is located next to the phrase "Apply Palette to App Icons."

Also, take into consideration that the availability of this palette option could differ depending on the app icon you're using.

CHAPTER SIX

Adjust display's settings

Users of Samsung tab S9 have access to a wide variety of display customization choices, which ensures that their experience may be molded to suit their individual preferences. You have the ability to customize a variety of things to meet your requirements, including the text size, the size of the content that appears on the screen, as well as the color settings and the white balance.

How to customize your font size and style

Your eyes are starting to become tired from staring at the screen for so long since you are so fascinated in the fascinating new blog that you have been reading. You could try adjusting the font settings to relieve this problem and give your eyes the rest they so richly deserve.

These are the adjustments that need to be made:

- Launch the menu for the Settings.
- Proceed to the next section, which is called **Display.**
- Locate the option to change the font size and style, then tap on it.
- After that, you'll be able to customize the font settings to your specific preferences.
- Tap the **Font style option** if you want to choose a different typeface to use.
- Check out the Download fonts option to broaden your selection and have access to even more fonts to choose from.

Your reading should become more pleasant and easy on the eyes as a result of these straightforward alterations, which should be made.

Enable Screen Zoom

You can make use of the Screen Zoom tool to magnify the text that is displayed on your screen, which is extremely helpful while you are reading articles.

- Launch the settings menu on your device, and then select "Display."
- Scroll to the bottom and click the "Screen Zoom" button.
- Utilize the slider at the bottom of the screen in order to make adjustments to the zoom level.

How to turn on Full Screen apps

Increasing the amount of space available for the thumb would make the process of improving the gaming experience much simpler, while increasing the size of the screen would improve the experience of watching videos. Verify that the application you're using supports operating in full-screen mode.

To make use of this function, please proceed as follows:

- Enter the Settings menu, then tap the **Display option.**
- Proceed to **the Full screen apps menu.**
- To make maximum use of your device, enable full-screen mode by toggling the switch that is located next to the app you want to use.

Adjust color settings

Note: Depending on the model of your device, the screen modes may be different or completely absent.

Does it look like the image has been distorted? Screen Mode and color options both allow you to modify the appearance of the display to your liking.

- To get started, pick **Display** from the menu **under Settings**, and then hit the **Screen Mode button**.
- Now, select the screen mode that best suits your needs. Be advised that turning off the **Blue Light Filter** may be required in order to access some screen modes.

How to use Easy Mode

Consider turning on Easy Mode if you're having trouble finding your way around your Home screen and need some assistance. This feature will increase the size of on-screen items, provide a keyboard with a high contrast, and decrease the likelihood of accidentally touching the screen while tapping.

The following procedures need to be taken in order to activate Easy Mode:

- Launch the **Settings menu** on your device.
- Choose the **Display option.**
- Find the Easy Mode option, and then hit it.
- To make it work, you need to flick the switch.

Adjust your screen brightness

The sun is shining quite brightly today, making it difficult to view the screen on your device. You need not be concerned, though, as there are several adjustments you may make to the level of brightness.

- To begin, go to **the Settings menu** and then select **Display** from there.
- You can adjust the brightness of the screen to your personal preference using the bar that is located there.

You have the option to turn on or turn off the **Adaptive Brightness feature** if you would rather have a solution that is more automatic. This handy function adjusts the brightness of your device based on the conditions in the surrounding area. Tap the switch that is located next to Adaptive Brightness in order to turn the feature on or off.

In addition, the panel that contains the **Quick Settings** allows you to easily adjust the brightness of your screen. Using two fingers, swipe down from the top of the screen, and you'll find a slider at the bottom of the panel that enables you to make immediate modifications.

How to make streaming videos look best

Note: Depending on the model of your device, the screen modes may be different or completely absent.

Take full advantage of the outstanding screen capabilities of your Samsung Tab S9 series! The majority of streaming applications can now benefit from the Video Enhancer feature's seamless integration, which results in colors that are more vivid and striking.

- To make use of this function, go to the **Settings menu**
- Afterwards, pick the **Advanced Features option**
- And then touch the **Video Brightness button.** In this section, you have the option of selecting either the Normal or Bright mode.

In the event that you select the Bright mode, an inventory of the applications that are compatible with it will be shown to you. To pick the applications that should get the automated upgrade, you need only to toggle the switches.

Additional video settings

Your Tab S9 series provides you with a variety of additional features and adjustment options that can improve the quality of your experience. If your Home screen appears congested, for instance, you may clean it up by arranging your apps and other stuff in a more organized fashion.

Do you feel like you have a headache after staring at a screen for too long? You have the choice to either lessen the amount of strain placed on your eyes by activating the Dark mode or the Night mode, or you can modify the screen refresh rate to provide a more comfortable viewing experience.

CHAPTER SEVEN

Take a screenshot

Whether you've just reached a new level in a game or you need to save an important document, you can easily record it by taking a screenshot on your Samsung Tab S9. This feature is available on both Android and iOS devices. It's possible that the procedure of taking a screenshot will be slightly different depending on the device that you use; nonetheless, taking screenshots is still a basic and time-efficient way to save photographs on your device.

Also, bear in mind that the screens and settings that are available to you may vary depending on the device model, the software version, and the wireless service provider that you use. It is also important to note that when you are using the Secure Folder mode, the screenshot feature might not be available to you. This is something to keep in mind.

How to use button combinations

The process of taking a screenshot on a Tab s9 Series, is very identical, with the possible exception of the button placements, which can be slightly different depending on the device. You will first need to locate the Power key and the Volume Down button in order to start taking screenshots.

In most cases, the Power button (or Side key) will be located on the right side of the device, while the Volume buttons will be located on the left side. It is important to keep in mind, however, that the positions of these keys might be switched on some models, or that all the buttons might be clustered on the same side of the device on other types.

- To take a screenshot, simply hold down the Volume Down key as well as the Power key (or Side key) at the same time, and then releases both keys simultaneously.
- When the screen flashes briefly, letting you know that the screenshot was successfully

taken, you will know that it was taken successfully.

How to use Palm swipe

"Are you aware that there is another way to take a screenshot besides the one you've been using? You don't have to click any buttons on some devices because they have a feature called Palm swipe that lets you take a screenshot with just a swipe of your finger.

- To make use of this function, open the **Settings menu** on your device,
- After that, conduct a search for "Palm swipe to capture," and then make that option your default.
- Next, tap the switch that is situated next to 'Palm swipe to capture.'
- Once it is engaged, you will be able to easily capture a screenshot by dragging the edge of your hand across the screen of your phone.

How to use voice to take screenshot

You can quickly take screenshots with voice commands if you have Bixby Voice or Google Assistant set up and enabled on your device. Simply utter the command, "Hey Bixby, take a screenshot," and the virtual assistant will immediately do its job. You are even able to send more complex requests, such as "Hey Bixby, take a screenshot and post it on Twitter."

You can also use Google Assistant to capture screenshots by just saying, "Hey Google, take a screenshot." This option is available if you like to use it.

How to use S pen to take screenshot

Our S Pens are compatible with a diverse selection of smartphones and tablets from the Galaxy line. Screenshots can be easily captured with the Screen write functionality, in addition to the countless other functions and capabilities that come included with these products.

These are the steps you need to take in order to take a screenshot:

- Take out your S Pen and put it somewhere safe.
- Proceed by navigating to the particular screen that you want to capture.
- Tap the icon representing the Air command menu with your S Pen.
- To write on the screen, select "Screen write."
- Your device will take a screenshot of the page that you are currently viewing automatically.
- Make use of the controls that are offered in order to write or draw on the snapshot as you see fit.
- After you have achieved the desired result, select the Save option to save the snapshot to your Gallery.

How to use Tasks Edge panels

Taking screenshots on your device can be made much simpler with the assistance of the Edge panel. Follow these steps to get this up and running:

- To access the Edge panel, select the handle on the right side of your screen and swipe left across it.

- Tap the Settings icon in the bottom-right corner, then scroll up until you reach the **Tasks panel** and pick it.

- Tap the **Edit button** located in the Tasks panel. You can access the shortcuts that you prefer on the right side of the screen. To add "Take screenshots" to your list of shortcuts, swipe all the way to the left and hit the button. Please take into consideration that this shortcut might already have been introduced automatically.

- You also have the opportunity to personalize your shortcuts by picking and choosing which extra items to include or exclude. Tap the minus sign in the upper-right corner of the screen to delete a shortcut.

- Keep in mind that the total number of shortcuts you have access to cannot exceed "twelve."

- After you have completed the configuration of your shortcuts, proceed to the screen that you wish to record.

- To access the Edge panel handle once again, swipe to the left on the edge of the screen. You'll need to swipe left one more time to go to the Tasks panel.

- To capture a screenshot, select "Take screenshot" from the Tasks menu. Your device will immediately take a screenshot of the currently active screen. When you need to take a screenshot of your computer screen in the future, you can take use of this time-saving shortcut!

How to use scroll capture to capture more than one screen

Is there too much content on the website to fit into a single screenshot? Scroll capture enables you to take many screenshots of a single page, and it then combines all of those images into a single, full picture. Because of this, you will be able to record the complete content.

In addition, scroll capture may be combined with various methods of taking screenshots, such as button combinations, palm swipes, or even the S Pen, for a seamless integration. Therefore, regardless of the approach that you favor, scroll capture will always be a choice that may be made.

This is how you should put it to use:

- Find the portion of the screen that you want to capture and click it.
- To capture the screenshot, you can use any one of the ways that were discussed earlier.

- When the Smart capture menu displays, look for an icon that resembles a downward arrow and tap on that symbol. The icon will animate by bouncing up and down.

- To begin the process of scroll capture, you will need to tap the icon a second time.

- Keep touching the icon until you get to the bottom of the page or the place where you want to stop, whichever comes first.

- You have the option of adding tags to your screenshots by tapping the hashtag icon located in the menu under Smart capture. You have the option of using the suggested tags or coming up with your own. To store your selected tag, use the "Save" button.

- When you are finished, you can exit the Smart capture menu by simply tapping outside of the bar. You can view the screen that was captured by either tapping the screenshot preview or going to the Gallery.

Note that the Smart capture indicator will only appear while you are viewing a large web page, app screen, or image that requires scrolling. This is the only circumstance in which it will be displayed. It's possible that certain websites won't support it.

How to view screenshots

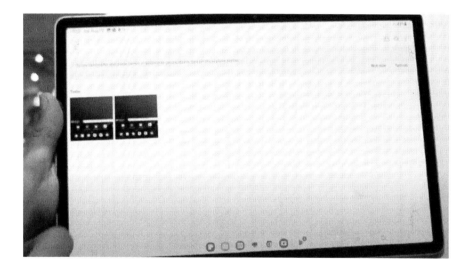

You are able to access your screenshots quickly and easily from a centralized location, regardless of the device(s) you use. Simply access the app by going to your Gallery on your device. You also have the option of tapping the screenshot notification after revealing the notification panel by swiping down from the top of the screen. This will bring up the notification panel.

- You can find a collection of all the screenshots you've saved on some devices under the **Albums page in** the Gallery app. This tab is located on certain devices.

- You have the option of using **the My Files app** to gain access to your screenshots, in addition to your films, documents, and downloads, if you would like another method. Launch the My Files app, then navigate to the Images menu and select it to view your screenshots.

- You can take the additional step of storing your screenshots on a microSD card, an OTG flash drive, or your personal computer if you want to prevent your Gallery from becoming cluttered with an excessive amount of photographs. You can choose from a number of different methods to transfer your screenshots, such as making use of the My Files application to copy them onto a microSD card. This contributes to the organization of your device and helps keep your Gallery clear of clutter.

How to share screenshots

When you finally beat that challenging level in your brand-new game, make sure to show your friends and family how proud you are by sending them a screenshot.

- To quickly share a screenshot after taking it, simply slide down from the top of your screen to display the notification panel. This will allow you to quickly share the screenshot. Find the notification about taking a screenshot, and then tap the icon with the arrow pointing down. After that, choose "Share" and then select one of the many available choices for sharing the content.
- You can use the Gallery app to save the screenshot to your device for subsequent sharing if that's more convenient. Proceed to

the "Albums" menu, and from there, select "Screenshots." To take the screenshot you want, simply press and hold the selected screen capture for a few seconds, then tap the "Share" button.

Additional options

When taking a screenshot, you have access to a few additional choices, including the capability to alter the snapshot and give it a more personalized feel as a result of your changes.

As soon as you take the screenshot, a pull-down menu will appear at the very bottom of the screen. To annotate or draw on the screenshot, all you have to do is select the "Edit" option (represented by a pencil icon). You can also crop out any areas of the screenshot that aren't essential. Your Gallery will immediately be updated to include the cropped portion of the image.

CHAPTER EIGHT

Samsung Health

There are ways to make **Samsung Health** even more functional than it now is, despite the fact that the app itself is already quite outstanding. To begin, the app can be synchronized with your smartphone and other Samsung Health-compatible devices. Some examples of these products include fitness bands, smartwatches, headphones, and some types of smart TVs. Because of this integration, you will have an easier time sticking to a regular exercise schedule.

In addition, you are able to link all of your favorite fitness applications to Samsung Health in a streamlined manner, which will enable you to access all of your health-related data in a centralized area.

How to view compatible accessories

If you are unsure about which accessories are compatible with Samsung Health, you can quickly find out which ones are compatible by browsing the accessories list that is conveniently located within the app. Using this list, which will supply you with information such as the product's name and kind, among which are smartwatches, heart rate monitors, and sensors, it will be very easy for you to locate the accessory that is most appropriate for your requirements.

Within the Samsung Health app, the following is the procedure for accessing the list of accessories:

- Launch the **Samsung Health app,** and then navigate to the app's primary screen.
- To access additional choices, use the three dots that appear vertically in the top right corner of the screen.
- Make your selection by clicking "Settings" in the dropdown menu.

- To view the available accessory goods, select the "Accessories" menu option.
- If you are requested, touch the "Allow" button to grant the permissions that are required.

The accessories will be organized into categories for your benefit, making it much simpler for you to locate the specific items that you require. To narrow down your search even further:

- To arrange the list in the desired order, pick the "Sort by" option and then choose one of the "Device type," "Manufacturer," or "Tracker" options from the drop-down menu.
- Make use of the search icon in order to locate a particular accessory in a hurry.
- You can also start a search for compatible accessories in the area by tapping the "Scan for accessories" button, which is available if you are looking for devices that are nearby.

How to add an accessory

Since you can't bring your Samsung Tab s9 series into the pool with you, you might want to consider syncing your smartwatch with Samsung Health so that you can keep track of how often you swim.

The Samsung Health app makes the process of connecting a new accessory a simple and basic one that can be completed with relative ease. It will instantly display as a registered accessory in Samsung Health if you have already paired and setup your Samsung device in the Galaxy Wearable app.

This is the procedure to follow:

- Launch the **Samsung Health app** and then tap on the icon depicted by three vertical dots to access additional options.
- Afterwards, navigate to "Settings," then select "Accessories."
- Make sure the device you intend to link it with is ready to do so. You will see a list of the many

device categories that are available. Find and choose your particular piece of hardware. If the type of your device is not one of those listed, you can select "Scan for accessories."

- Choose your device once it has been located and then proceed to follow the directions that appear on the screen to finish the setup procedure.

- Your registered accessories will be shown at the top of the page for your convenience under the heading "Registered accessories."

How to manage connected app permissions

Your experience of monitoring your health may be streamlined and brought together in a single, convenient location thanks to Samsung Health's seamless interaction with a variety of apps, including workplace wellness programs. If you've connected another app to Samsung Health, you'll have the ability to easily manage the permissions for that app and govern the data it can access.

This is the procedure to follow:

- Launch the **Samsung Health app** and then tap the icon that looks like three vertical dots. This will bring up further possibilities.
- Go to the **Settings menu.**
- Select **Applications**. You have the ability to view the permissions that are associated with connected apps inside this section.
- To allow or disable a permission based on your preferences, you can use the switch that is located next to the permission.
- After you have finished configuring the permissions, you can save your changes by tapping the **Done button.**

How to manage Services

While using Samsung Health, you have the option to share your health data with compatible services, such as some workplace wellness programs. The app contains information on all the services that are currently offered. It is possible that the service you are looking for is not compatible if you are unable to locate it. You are able to check the status of updates on a regular basis to see whether any new services have been added.

How to get access to these services is as follows:

- Launch **the Samsung Health app,** and go to the main screen when you get there.
- To access further choices, select the "More options" icon (it looks like three vertical dots) in the upper-right area of the screen.
- Make sure you select "Settings."
- You can examine a list of services that are compatible with your device by swiping down and tapping on the "Services" option.
- A list of the applications that may be found under "Services."
- To begin using a service, you need only to tap the switch that is located next to it. If this is your first time connecting to that particular service,

you will be prompted to either log in with an existing account or establish a new account.

- To detach from a service, simply tap the switch that is located next to it a second time to turn it off.

How to connect Samsung Health app and TV app

In order to provide you with an integrated health and wellness experience, Samsung Health can also be used on your television. Connecting your mobile app and any other accessories that are compatible with your TV, such as a Samsung Galaxy watch, is what we recommend doing in order to get the most out of this feature. Because of this, you will be able to manage your health and wellbeing across a number of different devices.

In order to accomplish this, the following requirements need to be met:

- In order to utilize Samsung Health on your TV, you will first need to make sure that your TV is logged in with the same Samsung account that you use for the Samsung Health mobile app, and then you will need to connect these two accounts. This is something that can be readily accomplished through the dashboard of the Samsung Health TV app.

- In addition, you can access the fitness content provided by Samsung TVs through the Samsung Health app that is installed on your mobile device. Launch the Samsung Health app, then go to the tab labeled "Fitness" to investigate the various pieces of content it contains.

Take into consideration the following suggestions before connecting your TV to Samsung Health:

- The information that is shown on the Dashboard receives an update whenever you begin a new session in which it is accessed, regardless of whether you are using the mobile app or the TV app. If you want to manually update your data, you can do so by clicking the refresh option, which is available to you.

- If you find that the data in the mobile app and the app on the TV are not same, check the timestamp on the TV to find out when the data were last successfully synchronized.

- If you want to disconnect the data from the mobile app, all you have to do is click the "Unlink" option from the Dashboard screen of the TV app or the mobile app.

- You have the ability to switch between profiles within the Dashboard by selecting the "Switch Profile" option that is found in the top right corner of the screen. This provides you with additional freedom.

CHAPTER NINE

Sync your Gallery photos with

OneDrive

You can trust Microsoft OneDrive to safely store all of your favorite images and videos, regardless of whether they are serious portraits or amusing selfies. You have the ability to set up your Gallery for automatic syncing with OneDrive, which will ensure that your files are simple to access anytime you feel the need to recall those occasions. In addition, OneDrive gives you the ability to restore photos and videos that you may have lost inadvertently.

Be advised that the availability of certain settings may vary depending on the software version that you are using as well as the carrier that you are using. In addition, support for this service is not available in every country or from every carrier.

Turn Gallery Auto Sync on or off

Take note: in order to begin using OneDrive for synchronizing your images, it is possible that you will first need to download the Microsoft OneDrive software onto your device and then link it with your Microsoft account. This is something that you should keep in mind.

It is possible that your Gallery app's Auto Sync option is set to be deactivated by default. Enabling it, on the other hand, is a simple process that will result in the synchronization of all of your images and videos with OneDrive once it is done.

This is how you can go about doing it:

- Open the **Gallery application.**
- To access the menu, select the icon that looks like three horizontal lines at the bottom of the screen.
- Make sure you select "Settings."
- To begin synchronizing, you need to turn on the switch that is located next to "Sync with

OneDrive." If you are currently in onto your Microsoft account but have not yet connected it to your Samsung account, the choice will be labeled as "Cloud sync." You will receive a notification asking you to sign in or link your Microsoft account if you haven't already done so. Simply comply with the directions that appear on the screen.

After you have enabled the OneDrive sync in the Gallery settings, the following will occur:

- Since the content of your Gallery will be synchronized with OneDrive, you will be able to access your photographs from other devices as well as the website for OneDrive.

As an alternative:

- Launch the OneDrive app on the device you're using.
- To view the photographs that you have synced, select "Photos" from the bottom menu.

Additionally, you have the ability to view photographs from OneDrive that have been synchronized with your Gallery app on your device. To accomplish this:

- Proceed to the app known as Gallery.
- Make your selection from "Pictures" or "Albums."
- You can locate the photos that have been synchronized from OneDrive in your Gallery with the other pictures you've saved there.

Following these instructions will allow you to sync your photos from Gallery to OneDrive in a way that is completely seamless.

Sync specific albums in Gallery

There are some photos that are more meaningful than others, such as pictures taken with your family while on vacation or selfies with your closest friends. You have the ability to pick and choose which Gallery albums will be synchronized with OneDrive, giving you the freedom to keep other albums stored locally on your device.

In order to get started with this procedure, follow these steps:

- Launch the Gallery app that's installed on your device, then tap on the icon that looks like three horizontal lines at the very bottom of the screen.
- Next, go to the **Settings menu,** and after that, select the option to Sync with OneDrive.
- Proceed to the Albums option found inside the Sync menu.
- By toggling the switch that is located next to each album, you will be able to select which albums will be synchronized with OneDrive.

Download photos and videos from

OneDrive

Photos and movies stored in OneDrive can be transferred to any other device, including mobile phones, tablets, and personal computers, with ease. If you wish to make a picture that's stored on OneDrive your phone's background image, you can do it by following these instructions within the OneDrive app:

- Launch the OneDrive app on the device you're using.
- You can either go to the Photos tab or directly to the folder that contains the file you want to access.
- Choose the picture(s) or video(s) that you want to save to your device and click "Save."
- To download, select the icon.

Confirm your selection by hitting the SAVE button, and the download of your file will start immediately. You can find it in your Gallery right there with the rest of your other pictures.

Delete Gallery files from OneDrive

It is simple to delete several images that you no longer require from OneDrive if you have a lot of them stored there. If, on the other hand, you would like to keep the images on your smartphone while removing them from OneDrive, you may do it by following these easy steps:

- Launch the **OneDrive app**, then go to the **Photos tab** in the menu that appears.
- Select the images that you do not wish to keep.
- To delete something, you need to tap the icon.
- Tap the **OK button** to verify that the deleted file was successful.

Restore deleted Gallery files from

OneDrive

Do not be alarmed if you find that you have inadvertently removed an image from your OneDrive; it is possible to retrieve it with very little effort. Your films and pictures are kept in a secure location in the Recycle bin for up to 93 days, giving you plenty of time to retrieve the file from that location. You also have the option of restoring deleted data straight from the website of your OneDrive account.

The following actions need to be taken in order to restore a photo that was deleted:

- Launch the **OneDrive app**, and navigate to your profile by selecting the "Me" tab when it appears.
- To access this option, click "Recycle bin."
- Look through the images in the Recycle bin to find the one you want to restore.
- To restore your backup, tap the "Restore" symbol that can be found in the top right corner of the screen (it looks like a clock with an arrow).
- Your photo will be sent back to its original location as soon as possible.

Note: It is important to avoid accidently tapping the "Trash" icon while a file is chosen, as doing so will permanently delete the file from your device.

CHAPTER TEN

S pen

Discover the effortless integration of Samsung's cutting-edge stylus pen with the most recent Galaxy Tabs. This stylus pen provides unrivaled power and precision in every gesture, creating an experience that is analogous to writing with a pen and paper. Dive into this chapter to learn how to use the Galaxy Tab S Pen with your brand-new Samsung tablet so that you can take advantage of its full potential.

How does the S pen work?

You now have the ability to interact with your new Samsung tablet in ways that go beyond the scope of standard touch controls thanks to Samsung's legendary S Pen stylus. You may express your creativity by writing, drawing, or swiping on the screen thanks to the pen's design that makes it seem like a genuine pen and its 4,096 levels of pressure sensitivity.

Simply removing the S Pen from its integrated holder on the back of your new Samsung tablet, hovering it over the screen, and starting to write will get your S Pen working so you can use it. In order to use the

S Pen to its full potential, you will need to activate **Air Command**, which is a revolutionary piece of software developed by Samsung that enables fluid interaction with your Galaxy Tab S9.

There is a vast amount of territory to cover when it comes to making use of your Galaxy Tab S Pen. You'll be a S Pen Pro in no time, whether you use it to write directly on the screen of your tablet, convert what you write to text, make and edit documents with Samsung Notes, or utilize PENUP to bring out your inner artist, because all of these features are available with the S Pen.

Explore the S pen features in Air command menu

Simply hover your S Pen over the tablet screen to access the Air Command menu, represented by a small circle with a pen icon. Within this menu, you'll find a range of options:

- **Create Note**: Begin writing and drawing using Samsung Notes.

- **Smart Select:** Utilize your S Pen to select and save content from the screen.

- **Screen Write**: Write directly on the current screen using your S Pen.

- **Live Messages**: Add a personal touch to your photos with animated GIFs, emojis, and handwritten text.

- **AR Doodle**: Exercise your creativity by drawing, annotating, and doodling on various surfaces using the S Pen in conjunction with the Galaxy Tab camera.

- **Translate**: Easily translate words or phrases by hovering your S Pen over them. You can also hear the pronunciation by tapping the sound icon.

- **PENUP:** Dive into drawing, coloring, and designing with your S Pen through the PENUP app.

How to draw Samsung tab S9

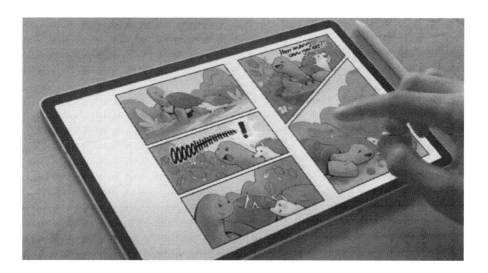

The exceptional Samsung stylus pen that comes standard with the most recent iteration of the Galaxy Tab makes it simpler than ever before to create and write on a tablet computer. You have a range of alternatives available to you, and you can choose to either increase the amount of work you get done or explore your creative side through the medium of digital art.

1. Smart Notes

- To begin using Samsung Notes, all you have to do is select 'make a note' from the Air Command menu on your device.

- Taking notes has never been easier. You can jot down notes, draw pictures, highlight text, change the size of the text, and play about with the transparency of the text all with the help of this tool.

- Once your work is finished, you can simply save it and share it with others.

2. Screen Write

Screen Write makes it simple to annotate photos, charts, or PDF documents. This feature may be found in the Air Command menu for your convenience. Following the selection of Screen Write, a screenshot of the material you are presently examining will be taken, and the S Pen annotation tools will immediately become visible. Because of this, you will be able to easily add notes, crop photographs, and communicate your thoughts via email or various messaging apps.

3. Screen off Memo

Have you ever found yourself suddenly remembering something? You may start taking notes on the screen of your new Galaxy Tab without having to unlock it by just removing the S Pen and beginning to write. In Samsung Notes, all of your previously stored memos will be shown in an orderly fashion.

Converting handwriting to text is a great option for those who find typing to be tedious. Place your S-Pen over the text field of any app that makes use of an on-screen keyboard, and then tap the handwriting symbol, which is represented as the letter 'T' in the icon's graphic representation. This enables you to write easily with the pen that comes with your Samsung device.

4. PENUP

When it's time to wind down and relax, turn to PENUP for a variety of creative ideas to help you unwind and relax. The S Pen allows you to learn how to draw, express your artistic flare through the creation of original drawings, or simply enjoy some thoughtful coloring on-screen.

All of these activities are possible. In addition, for those looking to take their creativity to the next level, the Galaxy Tab S8 series has collaborated with Clip Studio Paint, a painting app that is designed for professionals. Create works of art with your Galaxy smartphone serving as your paintbrush and the full Tab S9 screen serving as your canvas by using the S Pen.

CHAPTER ELEVEN

Tips of the getting the most of your device

The Samsung Galaxy Tab S9, the Samsung Galaxy Tab S9+, and the Samsung Galaxy Tab S9 Ultra are the most recent additions to Samsung's lineup of Android tablets. These tablets are designed to improve the efficiency of corporate operations. If you are considering making an investment in these gadgets, you might be interested in some helpful advice on how to make the most of the extensive variety of capabilities they offer.

The Tab S9 family of tablets has been painstakingly developed to facilitate uninterrupted work whether you are moving around or working from the comfort of your own home office. All three versions come with the Snapdragon 8 Gen 2 CPU, which provides the necessary performance and efficiency for effective multitasking. There will be less of a need for standalone desktops or laptops as more connectivity options such as Wi-Fi 6E and 5G are incorporated.

These tablets may be transformed into laptops with the help of extra keyboard shells, and they also come equipped with Samsung DeX capability, which creates an environment similar to that of a personal computer so that you can access your mobile applications. Additionally, the Galaxy Tab S9 may be easily connected to a monitor or television, enabling DeX mode on a larger display while still allowing you to use your tablet concurrently. This feature is exclusive to the Galaxy Tab S9.

In addition to these functionalities, the Galaxy Tab S9 family of tablets is equipped with a wide variety of features that are meant to make your professional life easier. Interested in learning more about the features of a Samsung tablet? Explore the following hints and tips for the Samsung S9 tablet, which explain how to make the most of the device's capabilities:

Take advantage of the large display to maximize multitasking

Power users, who are typically people who generate and provide information to their customers, have traditionally relied on their laptops because of the larger screens available on these devices. However, the Tab S9 Ultra provides a more practical and transportable alternative with its amazing 14.6-inch display, which is on par with the size and visual experience of the majority of laptops.

Because of this characteristic, it is especially well-suited for professionals working in a variety of different industries. For instance, companies working in the financial services industry can use it to more effectively market their goods and services to customers using the platform. Retail staff can use it to create captivating mood boards for clients, and healthcare experts can use it to discuss treatment information in a safe environment.

In addition, the cutting-edge Dynamic AMOLED 2X display technology is utilized across the board for Samsung Tab S9 products, and these products now come equipped with the Vision Booster feature. This cutting-edge function automatically adjusts the display's brightness whenever the device is used in natural light, making it suitable for usage in a wide range of environments with varying levels of illumination.

Mark up documents and control your tablet with the S Pen

One of the best aspects of the Tab S9 series is that it comes included with the S Pen, which can be purchased separately if desired. When you remove the S Pen from its holster on the rear of the tablet, the Air Command menu is activated, giving you speedy access to a variety of settings and options.

Because of this user-friendly experience, converting handwriting to text seems astonishingly comparable to writing on paper. This sensation is heightened by the app's compatibility with professional-level software such as GoodNotes.

Whether you're giving a presentation or taking photos, you can use Air Actions to provide yourself seamless control with the use of gesture commands with your S Pen. These actions can be modified in the Settings app under the section titled "Air Actions," whether it be forwarding slides in a presentation or zooming in while using the camera.

A straightforward magnetic attachment to the rear of your tablet makes it possible to quickly recharge your S Pen whenever its power supply is running low.

See it all at a glance with Multi-View Windows

Your productivity will skyrocket once you start using the Multi-View Window layouts on your tablet, which will enhance your ability to multitask. This feature grants you the ability to display four separate layouts concurrently on your screen, providing you with unequaled versatility by enabling you to modify the height and width of each configuration. You are no longer limited by fixed a layout, which means you may easily switch between various apps and take notes while simultaneously participating in video conferences without any difficulty. In addition, Tab S9 devices come equipped with the practical functionality of a split screen, which enables users to see previously viewed content on a single page while simultaneously browsing additional content in a split view.

Add the 2-in-1 Book Cover for laptop-like productivity

The Tab S9 series provides agile computing solutions along with displays that support interactive touch interactions. Nevertheless, if you want a full-sized tactile keyboard, the sophisticated 2-in-1 Book Cover is a product that you should think about purchasing.

It provides keyboard capabilities similar to that of a PC, complete with keys that are completely backlit and simple shortcuts for accessing your preferred applications or DeX. In addition to this, you can effortlessly share your wireless keyboard between your phone and your Tab S9 Ultra in a completely hands-free manner.

The **Book Cover** also features a variety of standing modes, giving you the ability to tailor it to the exact activities you need to complete. In addition, its intelligent functionality ensures that your screen reacts to whether or not the cover is open by turning on or off appropriately depending on the state of the cover.

Use Samsung DeX, wired or wirelessly, on an external display

You are no longer restricted by the limitations of your S9 tablet thanks to the adaptability of Samsung DeX. You are able to effortlessly project your work onto a larger screen since you have the option to connect using a USB-C to HDMI connection or to link seamlessly to a wireless display that is enabled with Miracast.

This is a new level of convenience in parting ways with your laptop, all thanks to DeX. Whether you're sharing dynamic presentations with coworkers in the same location or hoping to enhance your productivity with an expansive monitor that accommodates all of your mobile apps, this offers a new level of convenience in parting ways with your laptop.

Ensure you've got the connectivity you and your team need

The criteria for connectivity that are placed on business users might vary greatly from one department or job to another. All three S9 devices enable Wi-Fi 6E speeds of up to 2.4Gbps, which is approximately double the speed that was available in earlier models. These speeds are available to individuals who are working either remotely or within the workplace.

It may be necessary for employees to have flexible connectivity in some circumstances in order to keep up their productivity regardless of where they are, whether they are in a car or at a remote location. This is where the connectivity offered by the Tab S9+ 5G comes into play, which provides connections that are both even quicker and more secure than in the past.

Connect to higher-quality video calls more quickly

We've all had a good laugh at those video calls that freeze up or make us squint to hear what the other person is saying, but the fact of the matter is that every group needs an approach to online communication and collaboration that is basic and effective.

Because Samsung has formed strategic collaborations with other industry giants such as BlueJeans by Verizon and Cisco WebEx, it has been able to integrate calling services on Tab S9 devices in a way that is completely seamless.

For example, if you're using BlueJeans, you can easily mute your microphone, adjust the settings of your camera, or end your call with a single button push or even an air gesture with your S Pen. These actions can all be performed on your device.

Keep everything safe with Samsung Knox

Through the use of Samsung Knox, the Tab S9 series provides a high level of security, which is essential for the protection of sensitive information such as financial data and personal details. This platform offers complete data protection, covering not only the hardware but also the software levels. For example, Knox Vault assures that data does not become susceptible to breaches caused by physical attacks, fault injection, or side panels. This is accomplished by storing the data in a location that is resistant to tampering and providing a secure channel that is exclusive to the system between the CPU and the memory.

Using the function known as Secure Folder can provide an additional layer of protection for your files. By utilizing a personal identification number (PIN) or a pattern, this function provides you the ability to provide an additional degree of protection for private information. In addition, Samsung Message Guard enhances security by reducing the number of vulnerabilities that are caused by the many permissions required by messaging apps.

The Tab S9 series provides bio identification with the use of a straightforward on-screen fingerprint scanner, which makes the process of unlocking the device both simple and safe. These tablets also come with continuing protection and support, including access to four generations of One UI and Android OS upgrades, as well as a promise to deliver security updates for a period of up to five years.

Effortlessly share information across connected devices

The Galaxy Connected Experience is available on all the Tab S9 models, which means that you can employ features like Quick Share to easily transfer files or photographs from your tablet to your smartphone or other compatible devices. In addition, you have the ability to make use of Multi-Control, which enables you to operate your smartphone through the use of your tablet. For instance, you might compose a text message through the use of the keyboard on your tablet. The Auto Share tool gives you the ability to record videos on your phone, after which you may easily edit them on your tablet.

Due to the fact **that Buds Auto-Switch** eliminates the necessity of manually disconnecting and reconnecting the headphones, switching from listening to a podcast on your phone to watching a video on your Tab S9 is a breeze. In addition, the enormous display of the Tab S9 Ultra may be used in conjunction with your smartphone to provide a more immersive visual experience. This is made possible by the device's ability to function as a useful second screen.

Get more done with pro-level and B2B-specific apps

In addition to its compatibility with GoodNotes, which was discussed earlier, the Tab S9 provides smooth integration with ArcSite, which is a vital tool for rapid and effortless CAD sketching. This is particularly beneficial for professionals working in industries such as manufacturing, where such capabilities are extremely useful.

In addition, the Tab S9 is an amazing device for successful project management via applications such as Wrike, in-depth analysis of email marketing campaigns via Zoho Campaigns, and efficient organizing of your digital workspace with Notion. All of these capabilities can be found on your tablet. Last but not least, make sure you investigate Folia, a multifunctional platform that is perfect for collecting insights by annotating documents with a S Pen, supporting collaborative work with coworkers, and sharing material across a variety of platforms.

CHAPTER TWELVE

Apps

You have the ability to explore and install a large variety of apps that are tailored to your preferences when you use the Samsung tab S9 series. These devices are adaptable app hubs. In addition, you have the ability to delete or disable applications that are no longer serving their intended purpose on your device. Acquainting yourself with the management of applications on your device will enable you to use all of its features.

It is important that you are aware that the screen layouts and configuration options may vary based on the individual model, the software version, and the wireless service provider that you choose.

How to Download apps

Both smartphones and tablets that use the Galaxy brand name offer access to not one but two app stores: the Google Play Store and the Galaxy Store.

With the Samsung Tab S9 series, you can quickly reach the Google Play Store by looking for it either on the screen that displays all the apps or in the folder labeled Google. On the other hand, you can locate the Galaxy Store either within the Samsung folder or directly on the screen that lists all the apps.

- To investigate the enormous catalog of available software, go to the app store that most suits your needs and make use of its searching and sorting capabilities.
- After you have located the application that you want, all you need to do is tap it, and then tap the "Install" button.

Also, be aware that the only apps that may be downloaded to your Tab S9 are the ones that are compatible with it.

How to Uninstall apps

If you want to uninstall an app that you don't use anymore, you can do so by following these steps:

- Swiping either up or down from the Home screen will take you to the screen that displays all of your installed applications.
- Find the application that you want to remove from your device and press and hold it.
- After that, select "Uninstall" from the list of available options.

Also, be aware that some of the preinstalled apps cannot be removed from your device in any way.

How to Disable preloaded apps

Do you have any apps that are preloaded on your device that you rarely use? You can disable these preinstalled apps, even if it may not always be easy to totally erase them from your device.

To accomplish this, go as follows:

- Swipe either up or down from the Home screen to access the Apps screen on your device.

- Find the application that you want to disable, then press and hold its icon.

- Choose the option to deactivate the application from the drop-down menu that appears.

It is important to keep in mind that some of the preinstalled apps cannot be removed permanently.

How to see which apps you've used recently

By pressing the **Recents icon** located on the Navigation bar, you will have access to your recent app history. Here, you will be able to view the apps that you have recently used as well as those that are presently operating in the background.

Follow these methods, however, if you want to find out how much time has passed since you utilized a particular app for the first time since you last opened it:

- Launch the Play Store app and select your profile image from the menu that appears.
- After choosing "Manage apps & device," the next step is to select "Manage."
- Make sure the tab labeled "Installed" is selected at the very top of the screen.
- Tap the "Sort by" icon that's located next to "Apps & games." This indicator can have a different label (such as "Recently updated" or "Size") depending on the filter settings that you have previously used.

pick "Most used" to view the applications you use the most, and pick "Least used" to see the applications you use the least frequently.

How to reinstall paid apps and themes

If you have already purchased an application or a theme, there is no need to purchase them again. Simply uninstall it and then reinstall it using the same account that you used to buy it in the first place.

Reinstalling Applications from the Play

Store

- Launch the Play Store app and select your profile image from the menu that appears.
- Choose 'Manage apps & devices,' and after that, select 'Manage.'
- Select "Not installed" from the drop-down menu that is located under "Installed."
- Find the application that you wish to reinstall, and then tap the Install icon (the down arrow) that is located at the top of the screen.

Reinstalling Applications from the Galaxy Store

In the event that you initially downloaded the application through the Galaxy Apps Store:

- Launch the Galaxy Store app, then tap the **Menu button** (it looks like three lines going horizontally).
- Go to 'My applications,' then from the 'applications' page, find the app that isn't there, then hit the icon that looks like a download button.

How to Hide and unhide apps

You have the option to hide an app if you want to get rid of it from the screen that displays all of your apps. This step will not remove the application from your device; rather, its icon will be hidden from display, which will prevent it from being selected inadvertently. If you subsequently decide that you want the app to be visible again, you may undo this operation and bring it back into view.

Follow these instructions if you want to hide or conceal an app:

- Keep your finger pressed down on a blank area of one of your Home screens.
- Tap "Settings" when you are finished.
- Swipe left to right until you locate the option to "Hide apps on Home and Apps screens," and then pick it.
- Now, select the application that you wish to conceal; if necessary, you can choose more than one application at a time. These applications will be displayed at the very top of the screen in the "Hidden apps" section.
- Tap the "Done" button once you have completed making your selections.

To unhide a hidden app, perform the following steps:

- Place your finger on an empty area of the Home screen and hold it there.
- Open the "Settings" menu on your browser.
- Select the checkbox next to "Hide apps on Home and Apps screens."
- By tapping the red minus sign, you can deselect the application that you want to bring back into view.
- To finish, tap the "Done" button. Your app will now reappear on the screen that displays all the available apps.

How to Manage app permissions

It's possible that an app will ask for your permission to view some information before allowing you to use certain functions. For instance, an email app may request permission to access your Contacts in order to import the contact information of your friends. If granted, this permission would allow the app to do so. You always have the ability to change the settings, even if you accidentally gave someone permission to do something.

- To continue, open the **Settings menu** and then select the **Apps option** from the submenu that appears.

- Find and click on the app that's relevant, and then go to the tab labeled **Permissions.**

- On the Permissions page, you will see options that are either authorized or Not authorized, depending on the circumstance. From this location, you will be able to modify your permission options in accordance with your requirements. You have the option of refusing access entirely, allowing access only when the app is being used, receiving permission prompts each time, or allowing access just while the app is being used. It is essential that you take into consideration the possibility that certain apps could provide you more options to choose from.

Also, keep in mind that Android includes a feature that will automatically reset permissions for apps that aren't being used and will then tell you that it has done so. When you run the appropriate application, you are presented with the option to reauthorize permissions at any time.

How to Change the default apps

Certain apps are responsible for doing particular duties in a consistent manner. For instance, if you have your device set up so that the Internet application is your preferred web browser, then clicking on a **hyperlink** will cause your device to immediately launch the Internet app. In the event that you want to alter these applications' default settings, you can do so by following these steps:

- Gain access to the settings of your device.
- Choose the "Apps" option from the menu.
- Also, select "Default apps."

In this section, you will be able to select the application that will serve as the default for a number of different categories, such as the web browser. To make changes, you need only pick the category whose settings you want to modify and then choose the application you want to use by default.

How to Check for app updates

Updating your apps on a consistent basis is required in order to ensure that they run smoothly. Either the Play Store or the Galaxy Store on your device might provide you with an easy method to update your apps.

Downloading updates from the Google Play store:

- Open the Play Store app and select your profile image from the menu that appears.
- Choose the option that says "Manage apps & device."
- Find the part that says "Updates available" in the menu.
- Locate the app that you want to update and then hit the "Update" button that is next to it. You can choose the "Update all" option, which is located in the top right corner, if you

would rather update all of your apps at the same time.

Updating the latest from the Galaxy Store:

- Launch the Galaxy Store app, then tap the **Menu button,** which is depicted as three lines running horizontally across the screen.
- To view new content, select "Updates."
- Find the application that you wish to update, and then press the "Update" icon that is located next to it. You also have the option of updating all of your apps at the same time by clicking "Update all" in the upper right corner of the screen.

How to Move apps to a microSD card

Consider moving your apps to a microSD card if the capacity on your Samsung Tab s9 series device is getting full from having too many installed apps, but you don't want to delete any of them. You will be able to continue use the applications in this way without placing further strain on your limited storage space.

CHAPTER THIRTEEEN

Settings and Connections

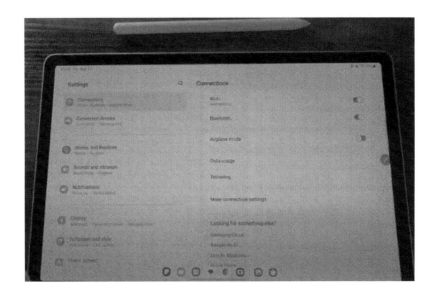

Wi-Fi

The Samsung Galaxy Tab S9 tablet series features a user-friendly interface that makes it easy to turn on the Wi-Fi connection. The following is a rundown of the procedures to activate Wi-Fi:

Unlock Your Tablet

If your tablet is locked, you can unlock it by entering your personal identification number (PIN), your password, or by using a biometric authentication method such as fingerprint or facial recognition.

Get in touch with the Quick Settings:

- To access the notification panel, swipe down from the top of the screen in any direction.
- You also have the option to swipe down with two fingers in order to gain access more quickly.

Find the icon representing Wi-Fi:

- Look for the icon that represents Wi-Fi. It has the appearance of an emblem representing the strength of a signal and has curving lines.
- To access the Wi-Fi settings, tap the icon that looks like a wireless network.

Activate the Wi-Fi:

- You'll see a toggle button at the very top of the Wi-Fi settings interface. It ought to say "Wi-Fi" next to a switch in the appropriate spot.

- To activate Wi-Fi, you need to tap the switch. When it is enabled, it will go from being grayed out to having a color next to it (typically blue).

Select a Network to Use:

- Your tablet will automatically search for available Wi-Fi networks once you have turned on the Wi-Fi feature.
- On the screen will appear a list of all the networks that are now available.
- Select the network to which you wish to join by tapping on it.
- In the event that a password is required, enter it here:
- You will be requested to enter the network password if it is necessary to protect the network with a password.
- To enter the password, use the on-screen keyboard that appears.

Create your connection to the Network:

- After you have entered the proper password, you will be prompted to hit the "Connect" or "Join" button (the terminology may differ depending on the version of Android you are using).

- Your tablet will make an attempt to connect to the Wi-Fi network that you have chosen.

Linked together:

- Once you have successfully connected, you will notice that the Wi-Fi symbol has changed to display signal strength bars, which indicates the strength of your connection.

That wraps it up! Since you have successfully linked your Samsung Galaxy Tab S9 series tablet to a Wi-Fi network, you are free to begin using online services or browsing the internet on the device. Make sure that you have the correct password for the Wi-Fi network if it is a secured network. If this is a network that you use regularly, you may also wish to configure your tablet so that it will automatically connect to this network in the future.

Bluetooth

Follow these instructions on a Samsung Galaxy Tab S9 series tablet in order to activate the device's Bluetooth functionality:

Unlock Your Tablet

- If your tablet is locked, you can unlock it by swiping it or by using your preferred means of authentication, such as a PIN, password, or fingerprint. If your tablet isn't locked, you can use either way to unlock it.

Access the Quick Settings Panel

- To launch the Quick Settings Panel, swipe down from the top of the screen. This will cause the Quick Settings panel to become accessible.
- Alternately, you can go here by swiping your finger down twice from the top of the screen.

Enable Bluetooth

- To turn on Bluetooth, go to the "Quick Settings" panel and look for the Bluetooth icon there.
- In most cases, it takes the form of a capital "B" composed of two triangular forms.
- Simply enabling Bluetooth requires a tap on its icon. The icon should change to a blue color when Bluetooth is turned on.

Optional Bluetooth options

- If you wish to access more Bluetooth options or link a new device, you can tap and hold on the Bluetooth icon or tap the text below it, which should state "Bluetooth."
- Either way, you will be sent to the Bluetooth settings screen. This will lead you to the page where you can configure the Bluetooth settings.

Device Pairing

- If you are connecting a new Bluetooth device, navigate to the Bluetooth settings page and select "Pair new device" or an option with a similar name from the list of available options.
- You finish the pairing procedure, make sure you follow the directions that appear on-screen.

Confirmation of Connection

- Once the connection has been estaⱱ.. the paired device will be displayed as an option inside the Bluetooth settings.

- You can modify the settings of the device or disconnect it when necessary by tapping on its name in the menu.

That wraps it up! You have been able to activate Bluetooth on your Samsung Tab S9 series tablet, and as a result, you are able to establish a connection with other Bluetooth-enabled devices, including headphones, speakers, keyboards, and more.

Data Saver

If you have a Samsung Galaxy Tab S9 series tablet and you want to get the most out of your data plan while minimizing the amount of data you use, activating and customizing the Data Saver option on your tablet can be an extremely helpful tool.

The Data Saver feature helps limit the amount of data that is used in the background, which enables you to maintain your connection without needlessly depleting your data allocation. In this section, we will walk you through the process of updating and optimizing your Samsung Galaxy Tab S9's Data Saver settings.

Access the Data Saver

- First and foremost, unlock your Samsung Galaxy Tab S9 device.
- To access the notification panel, drag your finger down from the screen's uppermost edge.
- To access the device settings, select the cogwheel-shaped "Settings" icon located in the upper right corner of the screen.

Locate the Data Saver and turn it on

- To access the connections, navigate to the bottom of the Settings menu and select "Connections."
- To access the Data Usage options, you'll need to tap the "Data usage" button.

Turn on the Data Saver

- You can find the "Data Saver" option within the Data Usage settings on your device. To activate it, you need to toggle the switch.
- When you turn on Data Saver, you will be presented with a concise rundown of how the feature operates. Read this to get a better understanding of the consequences it will have on the data use of your smartphone.

Modify the Settings of the Data Saver

- Tap "Data Saver" once again to get further configuration options for the Data Saver app on your Samsung Tab S9.
- You now have the ability to handle exceptions for specific applications. Even when Data Saver is turned on, certain apps are still able to make use of data in the background thanks to these exceptions. Tap "Unrestricted data" and then choose the applications from the list that you wish to be

exempt from the Data Saver's limits in order to add an exception.

- In addition, you have the ability to program Data Saver to activate on its own at predetermined intervals throughout the day by assigning it a schedule. To accomplish this, go to the "Schedule" tab and set the time range that works best for you.

Monitoring the Amount of Data Being Used

You can monitor how much data you're using by going back to the settings for your data consumption.

You'll be able to view a breakdown of your data usage by app as well as your overall data consumption in this section.

In order to prevent going over your data limit and going over your data plan, you should set up data warning and limit notifications.

If you follow these instructions, you will be able to efficiently manage and optimize the amount of data you use on your Samsung Galaxy Tab S9 series tablet through the use of the Data Saver feature. This will allow you to maintain your connection while extending the amount of time that your data plan covers and preventing any further costs from accruing.

Mobile Hotspot and Tethering

The mobile hotspot and tethering functions of the Samsung Tab S9 make it possible for you to share the internet connection of this tablet with other electronic devices, such as mobile phones, laptops, and other tablets.

When you are in an area that does not have Wi-Fi and you need to connect additional devices to the internet using the cellular data connection on your tablet, this feature can be helpful.

Installing and Configuring a Mobile Hotspot:

- **Open settings:** To access the settings on your tablet, swipe down from the top of the screen to reveal the notification panel, and then tap the icon that looks like a gear labeled "Settings."

- **Connections:** To configure your connection settings, go to the "Settings" menu and select "Connections."

- **Mobile hotspot and tethering:** To enable Mobile Hotspot and Tethering, go to the Connections settings on your device and press the option that says "Mobile Hotspot and Tethering."

- **Mobile Hotspot**: To activate it, tap on the "Mobile Hotspot" button.

- **Configure Hotspot:** This section allows you to make changes to the configuration of your hotspot. Altering the network name (SSID), establishing a password for the hotspot, and selecting the security type are all options available to you. These are the details that other electronic devices will need in order to connect to your hotspot.

- **Turn on:** To activate the Mobile Hotspot, simply flip the switch to the "on" position.

Getting Your Devices to Connect to Your Hotspot:

- Go into the settings for the Wi-Fi network on the device to which you want to connect.
- In the list of networks that are available, look for the name (SSID) of the hotspot that your Samsung Tab S9 creates.
- Choose the name of the hotspot, then input the password when prompted to do so.
- Once it is connected, the gadget will use the cellular data connection that is on your Tab S9 in order to access the internet.

Using a Tethering USB Cable:

- You can do this by utilizing a USB cable to connect your Samsung Tab S9 to the other device.
- To set up mobile hotspot and tethering on your tablet, follow the instructions listed in the

"Mobile Hotspot and Tethering" section located above.

- To activate it, you'll need to tap the "USB Tethering" button.
- Your device will display a notification to let you know that the USB tethering connection has been successfully established.

Utilizing Tethering via Bluetooth:

Establish a Bluetooth connection between your Samsung Tab S9 and the other device. In order to accomplish this, Bluetooth must be enabled on both devices, and then the devices must be paired via the Bluetooth settings.

- To set up mobile hotspot and tethering on your tablet, follow the instructions listed in the "Mobile Hotspot and Tethering" section located above.
- To activate this feature, select "Bluetooth Tethering" from the menu.

Keep in mind that tethering or using your tablet as a hotspot can cause your cellular data to be consumed, and the limitations of your data plan will still apply. When using these capabilities, it is strongly suggested that you keep an eye on how much data you are consuming so that you do not go over the restrictions of your plan.

More connection settings

The Samsung Tab S9 series provides a variety of connection settings to accommodate the numerous tastes and requirements of individual users. The following are some of these environments:

Wi-Fi

You can connect to Wi-Fi networks with the Tab S9 by visiting the "Wi-Fi" settings and following the on-screen instructions to do so. In this section, you will be able to browse through the available networks, connect to protected networks by entering their passwords, and even prioritize or forget networks.

Bluetooth Settings

The "Bluetooth" settings provide you with the ability to take control of all of your Bluetooth connections. This includes connecting your tablet to other devices, such as headphones, speakers, or smartphones, using the pairing feature. You also have the ability to manage linked devices and adjust the visibility of devices.

Mobile Hotspot

The Samsung Galaxy Tab S9 has the capability to function as a mobile hotspot, allowing you to share the device's cellular data connection with other electronic gadgets. This function may be accessed through the "Mobile Hotspot" settings, which are the same settings that allow you to set up the mobile hotspot, establish the security settings, and manage the devices that are connected.

Data Usage

The "Data Usage" settings provide you the ability to keep track of both your cellular and Wi-Fi data consumption. You have the ability to restrict the use of data in the background, set data limitations, and monitor use statistics for individual applications.

Near Field Communication (NFC)

The Samsung Galaxy Tab S9 is equipped with Near Field Communication, or NFC, which enables it to serve a variety of purposes, including contactless payments. The "NFC and Payment" settings are where you'll find the options to manage your NFC settings and turn on features like Samsung Pay.

Advanced Features

The "Advanced Features" section of the settings menu is where you'll discover choices such as "Quick Share," which enables you to quickly and simply exchange files with other devices in the immediate vicinity. There is also a possibility that you will uncover settings relating to "Direct Share," which allows you to share content with particular contacts.

Configuring Your Location

The "Location" options allow you to manage how your device interacts with location-based services. You have the ability to manage the location mode (high accuracy, battery saving, or device only), as well as app permissions for location access and recent location queries.

Connection Preferences

These settings give you the ability to modify how your device connects to various networks. You can select to automatically switch between mobile data and Wi-Fi, for instance, or you can activate options like "Wi-Fi Calling" if they are enabled by your carrier. Another option is to choose to automatically switch between mobile data and Wi-Fi.

Virtual Private Networks

Configuring Virtual Private Networks (also known as VPNs) can be done in the "VPN" settings section of the interface. When accessing the internet, having this functionality available is helpful for boosting both security and privacy.

Printing

The "Printing" options give you the ability to connect your tablet to various printers that are compatible with it, which enables the wireless printing of both images and documents.

Security and Privacy

The Samsung Tab S9 Series offers a huge breakthrough in tablet technology, providing users with an experience that is both adaptable and powerful when it comes to computing. In addition to its remarkable features and capabilities, Samsung places a significant emphasis on security and privacy to ensure that your data will always be secure and that your personal information will be safeguarded. The following is a list of important components of the Samsung Tab S9 Series' security and privacy features:

Knox Security

The well-known Knox security framework developed by Samsung is incorporated into the Tab S9 Series. Your device is protected from the hardware all the way up to the software level by Knox, which is a multi-layered security solution. It safeguards the system against malicious software, unauthorized access, and other possible dangers. You will have the peace of mind to use your iPad for both professional and personal purposes thanks to Knox.

Biometric Authentication

The Tab S9 Series comes equipped with a variety of innovative biometric authentication techniques, including as a fingerprint scanner and facial recognition. These ways allow you to unlock your device in an extremely handy manner while ensuring that it is protected from access by unauthorized parties.

Samsung Dex

When your tablet is linked to a monitor or TV, the Samsung DeX software enables you to have an experience similar to that of a desktop computer. Working on documents, navigating the internet, or running programs may all be done in a protected setting thanks to this feature, which separates your private information from what is shown to other people.

Privacy Controls

Samsung devices come equipped with a variety of privacy controls, some of which are app permissions, location settings, and a privacy dashboard. You have complete control over your personal information since you are able to simply review and manage the data to which your applications have access.

Secure Folder

The Secure Folder is a protected location on your Tab S9 where you can store sensitive files, images, and apps. You can access the Secure Folder by swiping left on the home screen. It is an encrypted environment that provides an additional layer of protection for your data by separating it from the rest of your tablet and adding another layer of encryption.

Regular Security Updates

Samsung is committed to providing regular security updates in order to fix vulnerabilities and safeguard your device from new threats. These updates should be installed on a regular basis. It is essential to your tablet's continued safety that you keep its software up to date at all times.

Private Share

Private Share is a feature that gives you the ability to manage the manner in which files are shared with others as well as the length of time that they are shared for. You have greater control over the privacy of your data thanks to the fact that you may give files expiration dates and even remove access after it has been shared.

Samsung Internet with Privacy Features

The Tab S9 Series comes with the Samsung Internet browser, which contains a variety of privacy features such as a built-in ad blocker, a mode for private browsing that is hidden from public view, and tracking protection.

Data Encryption

In order to safeguard the information that is kept on your tablet, Samsung implements a method known as data encryption. This assures that even in the event that your device is misplaced or stolen, unauthorized parties will not be able to access the data stored on it.

Multi-User Mode

If you share your tablet with other people, such as members of your family or coworkers, you can take advantage of the multi-user mode to create distinct user profiles, each of which can have its own collection of apps and data. This improves the level of privacy and security enjoyed by all users.

In summary, Samsung has made a great effort to guarantee that the Tab S9 Series not only provides top-tier performance but also places a premium on the safety and privacy of its customers by taking a number of precautionary measures.

You can use your tablet with complete peace of mind because it comes equipped with security measures such as Knox, biometric authentication, and privacy controls. In this way, all of your private information will be kept safe.

CHAPTER FOURTEEN

Troubleshooting

Let's look into some of the most prevalent problems that today's devices, in general, run into. If you happen to be experiencing any issues with your Samsung Galaxy Tab S9 device, you may relax knowing that I have created a detailed guide to assist you in resolving any problems that you might be having.

Let's get right down to business and solve the first issue right now.

Heating problem

If you encounter a heating problem with your Samsung Galaxy Tab S9 device, fear not. This issue is quite common and can be rectified with a few adjustments.

Addressing the Heating Issue

Here's how to tackle the heating problem on your Samsung Galaxy Tab S9:

- **Unplug After Full Charge**: Once your phone is fully charged, remember to unplug it promptly. Leaving it connected can often lead to overheating issues.

- **Opt for a Thin Back Cover**: Ensure you're using a thin back cover. Thick covers can hinder proper ventilation, contributing to heating problems.

- **Avoid Gaming While Charging**: Refrain from playing games while your phone is charging, and try not to use it excessively during this time.

- **Stick to the Original Charger:** Always use the original charger designed for the Samsung Galaxy Tab S9 when charging the device.

- **Limit Prolonged Gaming:** Extended gaming sessions are a common cause of phone overheating. Be mindful of this if you enjoy gaming on your device.

- **Avoid Unsupported Apps and Games**: Steer clear of installing unsupported apps and games, as they can also trigger overheating problems.

- **Keep Software Updated**: Regularly update both your phone's software and all installed apps to prevent potential issues.

- **Maintain Adequate Storage Space:** Don't let your phone's storage become overly full, as this can slow down the device and lead to heating problems.

- **Consider Ambient Temperature**: Keep in mind that your phone's environment temperature can also impact heating issues, especially in high-temperature settings.

- **Download from Trusted Sources**: Always download apps from the Google Play Store. Apps obtained from other sources can sometimes cause overheating problems.

- **Check Battery Health:** If your battery is old or in poor condition, it can be a significant factor in overheating. Consider replacing it if necessary.

- **Unlocking the Bootloader**: Optionally, you can explore unlocking the bootloader on your Samsung Galaxy Tab S9, but do so with caution.

Following these steps should help maintain your phone's temperature within acceptable limits. However, if the issue persists despite these efforts, don't hesitate to visit a service center for professional assistance.

Poor Battery life

If your Samsung Galaxy Tab S9 is experiencing rapid battery drainage, you can take the following steps to diagnose and resolve the issue:

How to Improve Battery Life on the Samsung Galaxy Tab S9:

- **Disable GPS When Not in Use**: Make sure to turn off GPS when you don't need it to conserve battery.

- **Uninstall Battery-Draining Apps**: If you've installed apps like phone cleaners, consider removing them, as they can consume battery power in the background.

- **Stick to Official App Stores**: Avoid downloading apps from sources other than the official Play Store to prevent potential malware from running in the background and draining your battery.

- **Use Default Settings:** Opt for general device settings instead of custom configurations, as custom settings can contribute to battery drain.

- **Monitor Battery Usage:** If you notice a significant drop in battery percentage, it may be time to replace your battery.

- **Adjust Screen Brightness:** Lower the screen brightness if it's set too high, as high brightness settings can lead to faster battery consumption.

- **Limit Gaming**: Playing intensive games can also drain your battery quickly, so try to minimize gaming sessions.

- **Check Recently Installed Apps**: If you've recently installed new apps and noticed a decline in battery life, uninstall any that claim to boost battery backup but may not be effective.

- **Avoid Prolonged Power-Saving Mode:** While power-saving mode can extend battery life, keeping it on for extended periods may cause the battery to deplete faster.

- **Consider Factory Reset:** If the battery problem persists despite the above steps, consider performing a factory reset on your Samsung Galaxy Tab S9.

Note: Ensure you have a backup of your important data before performing a factory reset.

After following these steps, you should experience improved battery life. If issues persist, don't hesitate to reach out to Samsung's customer support for further assistance. They can provide additional guidance tailored to your specific situation.

Sluggish User Interface

Are you finding that the user interface of your tab is sluggish and unresponsive at times? In that case, we offer a comprehensive solution that is tailored to your device. Before making any adjustments to your phone, be sure to follow these procedures very carefully:

Taking Care of the Lag Issues

1. Delete Any Unnecessary Applications

It is recommended that you remove any antivirus software or applications that clear up garbage from your device if you currently have them installed.

2. Make Room in Your Storage Area

Check to see that the internal storage of your phone has sufficient free space. If there isn't much room left, remove any useless files to make more room.

3. Conduct a search for malware

You should eliminate any possible viruses by connecting your device to a personal computer or laptop and running a scan with a reliable piece of antivirus software, such as Quick Heal.

4. Determine how fast the internet is.

A sluggish experience is sometimes the result of a connection to the internet that is too slow. Make sure you have a connection to the internet that is both reliable and quick.

5. If necessary, perform a factory reset.

If none of the aforementioned solutions resolve the problem, you might want to try performing a factory reset:

- Navigate to **the Settings menu**, then select **System**, then **Reset Options**, and finally select "Erase all data (factory reset)."

This has the potential to greatly enhance performance, but before you do so, you should back up any vital data.

6. Delete Any Apps That You Don't Use

You can free up system resources by uninstalling applications that you are no longer using.

7. Perform a Theme Analysis Again

There may be a performance impact from using custom themes. If you are using a custom theme, you might want to think about switching back to the default one.

8. Make Sure You Check Out Other People's Launchers

It is possible that the issue is a result of a third-party launcher that you just recently downloaded and installed. It is recommended that you uninstall it and use the system launcher instead.

9. Restart the Device You're Using

Check to see whether the issue is still there after doing a standard restart of your device.

10.   Perform Software Updates

Verify that your device is operating the most recent version of Android OS that is available. In that case, you can bring it up to date through the settings.

11.   Keep Your Apps Up to Date

The best way to ensure that all of your apps are running the most recent versions is to install any available updates from the Google Play Store.

If you follow these instructions, you should be able to fix the lag problem and have a more enjoyable time using your Samsung Galaxy Tab S9.

Camera Issues

The camera on the Samsung Galaxy Tab S9 has been acting up as of late, causing some significant problems. Users have noticed the camera suddenly turning off for no apparent reason, although the root of the problem is still unknown. You are in luck since there are actions that you can take to solve these issues, and they are as follows:

What to Do If Your Samsung Galaxy Tab S9 Has Camera Issues and How to Fix Them

- **Bug in Android OS**

With this issue, it seems that the root cause is a bug that exists within the Android operating system itself. You will need to wait for an official update to be released by Samsung in order to fix it.

- **Camera settings**

If you are having problems with the settings of your camera, one step that you can do to troubleshoot the issue is to reset the settings to their original, factory-default configuration.

- **Image Stabilization**

To get the most out of the capabilities of your camera, check to see if the Image Stabilization setting is on.

- **Clear Cache from Camera App**

In the event that the issue is not resolved, you should try emptying the cache from the camera app and then reopening it.

- **HD Option**

To improve the overall image quality, open the camera app's settings menu and select the HD option.

- **Reset the Camera Settings**

Whether you have made any personalized adjustments to the settings of your camera, you should reset them to their original state to see whether this solves the problem.

- **Elimination of the Screen Guard**

Sometimes, problems with the camera can be traced back to the screen guard. Take it out of the equation and check to see if the issue is still there.

- **Cleaning the Camera Lens**

In addition, if you are having issues with blurry photos, make sure to clean the camera lens on your Samsung Galaxy Tab S9 before taking any more pictures.

If you follow these instructions, you may be able to solve the problems that have been occurring with the camera on your Samsung Galaxy Tab S9 device. Remember to keep yourself apprised of any official upgrades that Samsung may roll out in order to guarantee a long-term solution to the issue.

Device shutting down unexpectedly

The Samsung Galaxy Tab S9, like other Android smart devices, is susceptible to unexpected power offs, which is a regular cause for concern. In the event that you are having this problem with your Samsung Galaxy Tab S9, the solution can be found in the steps that are listed below:

1. **Conduct a Battery Check on Your Device**

The first thing you should do is examine the state of the battery in your Samsung Galaxy Tab S9:

- Launch the dialer for the phone.
- After then, dial ##4636## on your keypad.
- To determine the current condition of your battery, go to the "Battery Information" menu option.

2. Keep an eye on the temperature readings.

Excessive heat might result in sudden shutdowns of cellular devices. In order to avoid this:

- Steer clear of utilizing cumbersome back covers that get in the way of adequate ventilation.

3. Free up internal Storage

Unexpected power outages can also be caused by insufficient available space within the device:

- Check how much internal storage space is still left on your device.
- Remove any applications or files that aren't needed to free up disk space.

4. **Carry out a Factory Reset**

If the problem still exists after executing the procedures outlined above, you might want to consider performing a factory reset:

Because taking this action will delete all the information stored on your device, you should only do it as a final resort.

- Make a backup of any vital data you have before continuing.
- Proceed to the settings menu on your smartphone.
- Locate the "Reset" option, then select "Factory Data Reset."

If you follow these procedures, you should be able to fix the issue with the unexpected shutdowns on your Samsung Galaxy Tab S9. Let's assume that the issue is not resolved despite your best efforts, it is recommended that you seek additional assistance from an authorized service center.

Screen frozen or stuck

Low random access memory (RAM) can be to blame when you find that the screen on your Samsung Galaxy Tab S9 has become unresponsive or frozen. When playing games, juggling multiple tasks, or making phone conversations, you could run into this issue. Take into consideration the procedures below in order to find a solution to this problem:

Troubleshooting Guide for Screen Freezing Up

1. **Ensure You Have the Latest Android Updates:**

To get started, check to see if there are any available Android updates on your mobile device. If there is an update available, installing it as soon as possible will ensure that your device continues to function normally.

2. **Application Cleaning:**

Find any applications on your device that aren't being used and either delete them or force stop them. By doing this, precious RAM space will be released, and the underlying problem may be fixed.

3. **Restart in the Safe Mode:**

Safe mode will need to be restarted on your Samsung Galaxy Tab S9 device. Check to see if the issue is still present. In that case, you should perform a normal restart of your phone and then uninstall the application that was causing the problem.

4. **Caution: Low Memory Level:**

Your screen may occasionally become unresponsive if there is inadequate free RAM or storage space on the device you're using. Make sure you have enough room to work without hindering efficiency.

5. **Troubleshooting Issues That Are Unique to the App:**

If you experience the problem while using a certain application:

- Go to the "Apps" menu, then select "See All Apps."
- Choose the app that's giving you trouble, and then erase its cache. This usually addresses any freezing issues that are peculiar to the app.

6. **Performing a Factory Reset:**

You can resort to doing a factory reset on your Samsung Galaxy Tab S9 if nothing else works. Because doing so will delete all of the information stored on your device, you should only resort to this option as a last resort.

7. **Custom ROM (Familiar Operating System):**

If you have previous experience customizing Android devices and have given the idea some thought, you may want to investigate the possibility of installing a custom operating system (ROM) on your Samsung Galaxy Tab S9. However, exercise extreme caution because doing so may void warranties and expose you to other hazards involved with modifying software.

In the vast majority of instances, insufficient RAM is the fundamental reason for the screen freezing. If you follow the procedures that were outlined above, you should be able to fix this problem and experience a more streamlined functioning on your Samsung Galaxy Tab S9.

Slow opening of apps

It's likely that you're familiar with the annoyance of having to wait for an app to launch on your device; this is a problem that affects many different kinds of products, including the Samsung Galaxy Tab S9. If you are experiencing this issue on your Tab S9, you can fix it by following these instructions in the following order:

1. Determine the Amount of Internal Storage That Is Available:

show

To get started, check to see if the device you're using has enough space on its internal storage. If you're getting low on space, you can free up storage by deleting useless files.

2. Optimize the Management of RAM

Sometimes, slow app opens can be related to inefficient management of RAM. This can be fixed by optimizing the management of RAM. Consider using a RAM Booster app in order to improve the overall performance of your device.

3. Uninstall Any Modified apps or Games

If you have any modified (Mod) programs or games loaded on your Samsung Galaxy Tab S9, you should uninstall them as soon as possible because it is possible that they are the source of the problem.

4. Reset Your Device

If the issue is still present across all of your apps, you should attempt to reset your device. Taking this one easy action can frequently fix performance-related problems.

5. Utilize the Lite Versions of Apps

If a Lite version of an app is available, you should switch to that version whenever possible in order to reduce the amount of RAM used and increase the speed at which apps open. These versions have been improved for a more consistent and seamless performance.

6. As a last option, execute a factory reset

If none of the procedures in the previous section are successful, you may want to consider performing a factory reset on your Samsung Galaxy Tab S9.

Always make sure you have a backup of your data before moving further with this option.

7. Get in Touch with Your Service Provider

Let's say that the issue is still present after attempting all the methods outlined above, it is recommended that you get in touch with your service provider or Samsung's customer support in order to receive additional assistance.

You should be able to address the issue of delayed app openings on your Samsung Galaxy Tab S9 by following these steps.

Games and apps crashes unexpectedly

It is really annoying when you start an application or game, only to have it quit on you unexpectedly. To our good fortune, this is a frequent problem for which there are readily available answers. To find a solution to this issue, please follow the instructions below:

Remove All App History:

- Find the app that's causing the problem by going to Settings and then Apps.
- Choose the application, and then delete all of its data.

Check the Amount of Storage Space:

- Make sure there is at least 1 gigabyte of free space in the internal storage of your smartphone.
- Delete the app and reinstall it.

It's best to uninstall the software that's causing the problem and then reinstall it; doing so will usually fix the crashing issue.

Keep the App up to date:

- Always make sure your apps are up to date by checking for updates in the app store and installing the most recent version available.
- Turn off the power saving mode as well as the safe mode:

- You should deactivate the Power Saving Mode and the Safe Mode if you've already enabled them, as these modes can sometimes cause app stability issues.

Carry out a check for viruses:

- To ensure that there are no problems related to malware on your device, you should perform a thorough scan using a trustworthy antivirus tool.

If you follow these instructions, you should be able to prevent the program from crashing in the future. If, despite this, you are still having problems, we ask that you kindly post a comment explaining the nature of the issue so that we may offer additional assistance.

Bluetooth not connecting

After turning on Bluetooth and attempting to connect with other devices, has your Bluetooth fallen out of sync and detached itself? If this is the case, simply follow the instructions outlined below to resolve any issues with the Bluetooth connection on your Samsung Galaxy Tab S9.

Problems with Bluetooth Connections and How to Troubleshoot Them

- Check to see that the "safe mode" setting on your device has been disabled.
- OTA updates, often known as over-the-air updates, are sometimes the cause of Bluetooth problems. Therefore, make sure you check for any updates that may be available.
- If you have previously modified the settings for your Bluetooth device, it is imperative that you reset those settings to their original state.
- Check to see that other phones will be able to discover your device.
- After turning off Bluetooth on your phone for a short period of time, you should then activate it again.
- Remove any and all devices that have been paired with your Samsung Galaxy Tab S9 in

the past, and then check to see whether the issue still persists.

- In addition, if you own a Samsung Galaxy Tab S9 and are interested in installing the TWRP (Team Win Recovery Project) Recovery software, you should be aware that the availability of the TWRP file may change depending on how far along the development process is.

You can ensure that your Bluetooth connection remains stable and continues to operate properly if you follow the instructions that have been outlined above.

Retrieving Information from a Display that Is Not Responsive on a Samsung Galaxy Tab S9

Problem: If the display on your Samsung Galaxy Tab S9 is damaged or the touch screen is unresponsive, but you still require access to your data, you should follow these steps:

1. **Establish a connection with your computer or laptop**

- Utilizing a USB cable, join your Samsung Galaxy Tab S9 to a desktop computer or portable computing device.
- As a result of this connection, you will be able to access the data on your device.

2. **Examine the microSD card.**

- If you have data stored on a micro SD card, you will need to remove the card and then reintroduce it into the device.
- Check to see if this fixes the problem and provides you with access to your data.

3. **Inspect the Screen Sensors**

- There is a possibility that the issue is caused by a faulty screen sensor.

- Conduct a visual inspection of the screen sensor to identify any obvious problems, and then take the appropriate action

4. **Access Applications Using an OTG Cable**

- You can use an OTG cable (also known as an On-The-Go cable) on your device in order to access its apps.

- Through the use of the OTG cable, you can link a wireless keyboard and mouse to your tablet.

- This configuration enables you to navigate and utilize your tablet in the same manner as a personal computer, giving you access to your data.

5. Diagnosing and Repairing Touch Functionality That Is Not Responsive

If the functionality of your touch screen is not working as expected, you can try the actions that were indicated above.

We really hope that following these procedures can aid you in recovering your data.

Wi-Fi and Mobile hotspot not connecting

If you're experiencing slow internet speeds on your Samsung Galaxy Tab S9 when using Wi-Fi, you can follow these steps to resolve the issue:

Potential Solutions for Wi-Fi Connection Problems

- **Weather Conditions:** Occasionally, adverse weather conditions can impact your Wi-Fi connection, especially during rainy or unpleasant weather.
- **Check Modem**: First, check if there's an issue with your modem. You can also consider resetting its settings.

- **Router Restart**: Try turning your Wi-Fi router off and on a few times. This simple step can often help improve connectivity.

- **Signal Range**: Ensure you are within the range of your Wi-Fi router. Being too far from the router is a common reason for a weak Wi-Fi signal.

- **Airplane Mode**: Toggle the Airplane Mode on your Samsung Galaxy Tab S9 for 2-3 minutes and then turn it off. Check if this resolves the problem.

- **Bandwidth Usage:** Verify whether you have exceeded the bandwidth limit of your internet plan. Overusing your allotted bandwidth can lead to slower speeds.

Additional Information: Rooting Samsung Galaxy Tab S9

If the Wi-Fi issue persists even after following these steps and trying different Wi-Fi connections, consider taking your device to a service center for further assistance.

By following these troubleshooting steps, you should be able to address slow Wi-Fi speed issues on your Samsung Galaxy Tab S9.

Resolving Cellular Network or Mobile Data Problems on the Samsung Galaxy Tab S9

Frequent cellular network issues can be frustrating when using any smartphone, and the Samsung Galaxy Tab S9 is no exception. If you find yourself experiencing signal fluctuations or poor connectivity, consider the following steps to address these problems:

- **Re-seat the SIM Card**: Begin by removing the SIM card from your Samsung Galaxy Tab S9 and then carefully re-insert it.
- **Airplane Mode Toggle**: If the issue persists, toggle Airplane Mode on and off after waiting a few seconds. This can sometimes help reset your network connection.
- **Reset Network Settings**: Another potential solution is to reset your network settings. This

action can clear any configuration issues that may be affecting your connectivity.

- **Check for Obstacles:** Signal interference can be caused by physical obstacles between your device and the nearest mobile tower. Ensure you are not in an area with such obstructions, as this can significantly impact your network reception.

- **Restart Your Device**: A simple device restart can often resolve network problems. After the restart, check if the issue has been resolved.

- **App-Related Network Issues**: It's possible that a recently installed app is causing network disruptions. Review your recently installed apps and consider uninstalling any that may be causing conflicts with your network connection.

By following these steps, you should be able to troubleshoot and potentially resolve cellular network or mobile data issues on your Samsung Galaxy Tab S9. If the problem persists, it may be advisable to contact your service provider for further assistance or consider checking your device for any hardware-related issues.

Apps not downloading

If you're having problems downloading apps from the Play Store on your Samsung Galaxy Tab S9, we can help. Rest confident that you are not the only user to have had this problem, and that there are several possible explanations for why it is occurring.

The issue where apps will not download or will download but remain in a pending state is frequently connected to recent modifications made to the Google Play Store. You can solve this issue by following the actions that are indicated in the following paragraphs:

Having problems downloading apps from the Play Store on your Samsung Galaxy Tab S9? Try these troubleshooting steps.

- Ensure that a reliable mobile data connection or Wi-Fi connection is available.

- Check the amount of free space that is currently available on your device.

- Check to see whether the issue is still there after you have restarted your Samsung Galaxy Tab S9 device.

- Check to see if there are any new versions of the Android operating system available:

a. Launch the Settings app on your device.

b. Select System > Advanced > System update from the menu that appears.

- In addition, you can fix the problem by erasing the local search history stored in the Play Store.

- Make an effort to delete all the app data associated with the Google Play Store. This step will almost always fix the problem when the app unroot your Samsung Galaxy Tab S9 if it becomes necessary to do so.

- You can also look into how to unroot your Samsung Galaxy Tab S9 if it becomes necessary to do so.

If you follow these instructions, you should be able to solve the problem successfully. Simply putting these procedures into practice whenever you run across this difficulty is all that is required of you, and I have complete faith that you will be able to address the problem.

Fingerprint scanner problem

The fingerprint scanner that comes standard on the Samsung Galaxy Tab S9 provides an additional degree of protection for its users. Despite this, a few customers have reported that their fingerprint scanners do not work as well as they had hoped. The topic of efficiently fixing this issue is discussed in depth in this section.

Problems with Fingerprint Scanners and How to Fix Them:

If that the fingerprint sensor on your Samsung Galaxy Tab S9 is giving you problems, there are a few different solutions that you can try in order to fix the issue, including the following:

- **Clean the sensor:** To clean the sensor, simply use a tissue or a soft cloth to gently wipe it down in order to remove any potential blockages or smudges that could be influencing its function. This is an easy process.

- **Reconfigure the Fingerprints:** Fingerprints must be reconfigured by first removing any fingerprints that are already registered and then re-registering them. This procedure has the capability of recalibrating the sensor, which has the capacity to get rid of any irregularities.

- **Software Update**: It is imperative that you always keep the software on your Samsung Galaxy Tab S9 up to date. It is recommended that you search for any available software updates and then install them, as these updates may include fixes for problems that are related to the fingerprint sensor.

- **Firmware Reinstallation**: If the same issues continue to arise, you may want to think about reinstalling the firmware that is related with the biometric capability of the device. This strategy has the potential to be successful in repairing the fundamental issues with the fingerprint sensor.

- **Seek Expert support** Let's say that the problem cannot be fixed, it is recommended that you get in touch with Samsung's customer service in order to receive assistance. Because of their knowledge, they are able to identify and fix particular problems with the fingerprint sensor on your device.

In conclusion, this chapter has given insights into the common issues faced while utilizing the fingerprint scanner on the Samsung Galaxy Tab S9, and more importantly, it has provided concrete methods to mitigate these concerns. Users can troubleshoot and finally repair difficulties with their fingerprint sensors by adopting these methods, which will ensure that their Samsung Galaxy Tab S9 tablets continue to function properly and maintain their level of security.

CONCLUSION

If you are looking for a tablet on the higher end of the spectrum, Samsung stands out as one of the limited alternatives available. The market is currently saturated with a plethora of budget-friendly Android tablets, but if you are looking for a tablet on the higher end of the spectrum, Samsung is one of the few possibilities available. If you have been eagerly expecting a challenger for the 11-inch iPad Pro, I feel you should give serious consideration to the Galaxy Tab S9 as an option. It has a screen that is outstanding, a design that is elegant and lightweight, a battery life that is remarkable, and a selection of accessories that can turn it into the ultimate portable laptop replacement you've always envisioned.

However, before you spend $800 on this tablet, it is essential to evaluate your personal requirements and preferences first. Do you feel comfortable using an LCD panel, or would you prefer a different type of display technology? Do you absolutely need a built-in S Pen, or are you able to live without one? Despite the large expenditure, are you prepared for the chance that your accessories can become obsolete after only one generation? These questions are really significant to think about.

Regardless of whether you care about functionality, if purchasing an Android tablet that is on par with a Porsche is your ultimate goal, I believe you will be more than pleased with what the Galaxy Tab S9 has to offer. If, on the other hand, your primary purpose for a tablet is to engage in activities such as endless binge-watching and scrolling through your many social media feeds — both of which are activities that are best suited for tablets — I would recommend you to investigate more cost-effective solutions that are better suited to meet these requirements.

ABOUT THE AUTHOR

Perry Hoover is a researcher, tech Entrepreneur, blogger and a technology writer, who is fond of blogging, technology research and writing. His areas of interest include Web application penetration testing, web security/architecture, cryptography, programming languages and database security. He is well versed with the latest technology, programming languages, computer hardware/software, and programming tools. He is also an expert in database security and application security architecture and penetration testing. He loves to share information about new technology and has published dozens of articles on it.

He has written articles on different aspects of IT Technologies including IT security, data storage and application development for magazines and has also published and co-published several e-books, of which the latest is on Windows 11. He has also worked with different private agencies to provide solutions to IT problems.

Perry Hoover

Manufactured by Amazon.ca
Bolton, ON

38162416R00140